HR's Role in Organising: shaping change

Professor Richard Whittington

Dr Eamonn Molloy

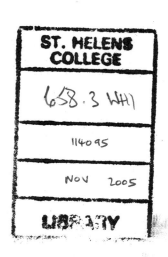
The Chartered Institute of Personnel and Development is the leading publisher of
books and reports for personnel and training professionals, students, and all those
concerned with the effective management of people at work.
For full details of all our titles, please contact the Publishing Department:

Tel.: 020 8612 6204
E-mail: publish@cipd.co.uk

The catalogue of all CIPD titles can be viewed on the CIPD website: www.cipd.co.uk/bookstore

For details of CIPD research projects:
www.cipd.co.uk/research

HR's Role in Organising: shaping change

Professor Richard Whittington

Dr Eamonn Molloy

Saïd Business School, University of Oxford

First published 2005

Cover design by Curve
Designed by Beacon GDT
Typeset by Paperweight
Printed in Great Britain by Short Run Press, Exeter

British Library Cataloguing in Publication Data:
A catalogue record for this book is available from the Britih Library

ISBN 1 84398 143 2

Chartered Institute of Personnel and Development
151 The Broadway, London SW19 1JQ
Tel.: 020 8612 6200
E-mail: www.cipd.co.uk
incorporated by Royal Charter: Registered charity no. 1079797.

Contents

Acknowledgements

The authors would like to thank Duncan Brown, Karen Giles and Vanessa Robinson at the CIPD for their support and input into this project. Also:

Evelyn Fenton *University of Reading*

Michael Mayer *University of Edinburgh*

Ann Smith *Open University*

The organisations that kindly contributed to the case studies used in this Final Report included:

CACHE

Cadbury Schweppes

Lever Fabergé

Lewisham Borough Council

National Health Service

Nationwide

Northamptonshire County Council

National Open College Network

Ordnance Survey

United Utilities

We would also like to thank the following members of the project's steering group for their contributions:

John Ainley *General Insurance, Norwich Union*

Chris Bones *Cadbury Schweppes/Henley Management College*

Dr Aysen Broadfield *GE Capital*

Andrew Campbell *Ashridge Strategic Management Centre*

Jane Cotton *Oxfam*

Andreas Ghosh *Lewisham Borough Council*

Chris Goscomb *RoyalDutchShell*

Jan Hutchinson *Ordnance Survey*

Dr Sheryll Kennedy *Kennedy Business Development*

John Lee *Martlet Business Services*

Dr Clive Morton *The Morton Partnership*

Andrew Newall *Allied Domecq*

Agnes Roux-Kiener *Unilever*

David Shaw *PricewaterhouseCoopers*

Mike Staunton *InBev*

David Smith *Asda*

List of figures, tables and case studies

Foreword

Organisational change is a regular feature of life, and for human resource professionals, dealing with reorganisations is now a regular part of the job. Given this situation, organising, ie the capability for repeated reorganisation, is what is increasingly important, rather than a particular, often transitory, organisational design.

There is lots of evidence that organisations are not very good at organising, and also that a more people-oriented approach, led by HR professionals, would improve both performance and also people's experience of re-organising.

Against this background, the CIPD embarked upon a three-year 'Organising for Success' research project in 2002. The research has been undertaken on behalf of the Institute by a team of researchers led by Richard Whittington, Professor of Strategic Management at the Saïd Business School, Oxford University.

The focus of the research has been on the 'how to' of reorganising, including:

◘ a review of current trends in organisational structure and design

◘ identification of current and emerging forms of organisation

◘ providing understanding of, and guidance on, the practice of organisational restructuring and the capabilities required for effective restructuring

◘ raising awareness about, and influencing practice in, effective organisational restructuring among senior executives

◘ analysing the contribution of effective people management for effective restructuring

◘ drawing conclusions and providing recommendations that support CIPD members in improving their contribution to the practice of organisational restructuring.

Since the project began three years ago, the CIPD has already published a series of research reports, surveys, executive briefings and articles, including:

◘ *Organising for Success in the Twenty-First Century: A starting point for change* (2002) by Richard Whittington and Michael Mayer

◘ *Reorganising for Success: CEOs' and HR Managers' Perceptions*. Survey Report, 2003

◘ *HR and Reorganisation – Managing the challenge of change*. A Change Agenda (2004)

◘ *Reorganising for Success: A survey of HR's role in change*. Survey Report, 2004

◘ *HR: Making Change Happen*. Executive Briefing (2004).

This is the final comprehensive research report from the three-year project and its purpose is to summarise the key learnings from the research, (drawing, in particular, on information from the two surveys and the 11 case-study reviews) and to draw out potential lessons from real life. In this way, we hope that it will help you to make an enhanced contribution to reorganisations.

We are very interested to hear your comments on these findings and how they compare with your own experiences, in order that we can continue to build our knowledge in this area. So, if you have any comments, please do let us know.

Vanessa Robinson
CIPD Adviser, Organisation and Resourcing
(v.robinson@cipd.co.uk)

Executive summary

This Research Report summarises key findings from a three-year research project funded by the Chartered Institute of Personnel and Development on 'Organising for Success'. The report focuses on the practical skills and capabilities required for undertaking reorganisations and similar organisational changes effectively. It builds on an extensive literature review, two surveys of senior managers and 11 case studies of major reorganisations, drawn from the private, public and voluntary sectors.

The Report focuses on reorganisations involving both changes in organisational structure and changes in softer features of organisations, such as culture. It shows that such reorganisations are an endemic part of managers' roles and that the pace of change is increasing. The report argues that today's relentless pace of reorganising requires a shift of mind-set: from looking for perfect organisation designs to building the skills and capabilities required for rapidly and repeatedly designing fluid forms of organisation.

Three central themes throughout this Report are:

1   The positive role Human Resource professionals can play in reorganisations as shapers of change.

2   The challenge of accumulating learning about change at the organisational level, rather than relying on the personal knowledge of a few key individuals.

3   The potential relevance of a core set of generic skills and capabilities across a wide range of organisations and sectors.

The Report identifies many skills and capabilities, but focuses particularly on what are called the 'seven steps to successful organising', based on statistical analysis of performance outcomes. These 'seven steps' point particularly to the importance of:

◻   sustaining top management support

◻   avoiding piecemeal, uncoordinated change initiatives

◻   achieving substantive, rather than tokenistic, employee involvement in the change process

◻   investing in communications with external stakeholders

◻   involving HR professionals closely, right from the start

◻   maintaining effective project-management disciplines

◻   building skilled change-management teams.

The Report concludes by discussing implications for HR professionals' training and development. If HR professionals are to rise to the challenge of shaping change, rather than simply sweeping up afterwards, they will need a wide range of skills and capabilities. Prime among these will be the ability to make a strategic business case, to situate any change initiative within the overall functioning of the organisation, and to employ sound project-management disciplines.

It is argued that the skills and capabilities required for a shaping role in reorganisations can be acquired through training and development within the HR functional career track. However, the example of successful change leaders and project teams from our case studies suggests that HR professionals need to combine knowledge and experience on their project teams from across organisations, sectors and functions.

1 | Why reorganisations matter

◻ The pace of reorganisations is accelerating, in both private and public sectors.

◻ In conditions of relentless reorganisation, organisational design skills matter at least as much as transitory organisational designs.

◻ Human Resource professionals are already highly involved in reorganisations, and need to take their place in shaping change.

Organising: responding to the pace of change

Organisation design is critical to organisational performance. At BP, chief executive Sir John Browne says: 'Our strategy is our organisation' (Day, 2001). The way in which an organisation is structured directly affects decision-making, accountability and coordination. Organisation design is tightly linked to central human resource domains such as careers, recruitment, training and reward.

The big challenge today is that organisations do not stand still. Indeed, the pace of change is accelerating, in both private and public sectors. Business organisations are increasingly entering a 'hypercompetitive' environment (D'Aveni and Thomas, 2005), in which competitive positions are constantly changing. The rate at which large companies in the United Kingdom are undertaking corporate-wide reorganisations increased from, on average, once every four years in the early 1990s, to once every three years at the beginning of this century (Whittington and Mayer, 2002). The public sector is under equivalent pressures for constant change. For example, in the last five years, the National Health Service has decentralised from the Department of Health, introduced primary care trusts, set up foundation hospitals, instituted strategic health authorities, established NHS Direct,

pursued the e-government agenda and instituted a major pay restructuring, the Agenda for Change.

These kinds of organisation-wide changes are the tip of an iceberg. Underneath these are a host of smaller reorganisations, such as mergers of departments or changes within particular business units. Including these smaller reorganisations, the average manager in our second research survey is closely involved in managing reorganisation initiatives once every two years (CIPD, 2004). HR professionals report even more reorganisation activity than average: 55 per cent of HR directors have been closely involved in three or more reorganisations over the previous five years. For HR professionals, dealing with reorganisation is now a regular part of the job.

Relentless reorganising

Change has become a way of working for the organisation.

> External report on Lewisham Borough Council, quoted by senior change manager.

Because we are in a competitive and dynamic market, restructuring and reorganising is set to become an inevitable part of life here.

> Senior change manager, major retail organisation.

The accelerated pace of reorganisations, and the wide impacts they have, entail an important shift in managerial responsibility. Organisation design is important, but any particular design is likely to be transitory. Increasingly, what matters is the capability for repeated reorganisation. Managers need to be skilled at designing and redesigning organisations on a regular basis, and organisations need to have the capabilities to handle and absorb this repeated kind of change.

> '... fewer than 40 per cent of reorganisations are meeting employee-related objectives such as employee morale and retention of key employees. Reorganisations are failing, and failing especially in the HR domain.'

These organising skills and capabilities are not yet well-entrenched in British organisations. Our first research survey of more than 800 CEOs, HR managers and other managers showed that, overall, only about half of reorganisations are meeting their objectives (CIPD, 2003). Reorganisations are most successful in meeting external effectiveness objectives such as increased market share or customer responsiveness, with 60 per cent reporting success. Slightly fewer are successful at meeting efficiency objectives or internal effectiveness objectives (such as knowledge-sharing). But fewer than 40 per cent of reorganisations are meeting employee-related objectives, such as employee morale and retention of key employees. Reorganisations are failing, and failing especially in the HR domain (Figure 1).

This mixed pattern of success sets a demanding change agenda, particularly for human resource professionals. A key argument of this report is that

HR professionals need to be proactive in shaping this agenda. Indeed, HR involvement in managing change is one of the 'seven steps to successful organising' that emerged from analysis of the second research survey (CIPD, 2004).

The 'seven steps' identify key factors associated with successful and unsuccessful reorganisations, based on post-reorganisation financial performance in private-sector organisations. We found that reorganisations are significantly less successful where they suffer from:

- a lack of sustained top management support;

- a piecemeal, rather than integrated, approach to change;

- tokenistic, rather than substantive, employee involvement.

Figure 1 | Post-reorganisaton performance outcomes

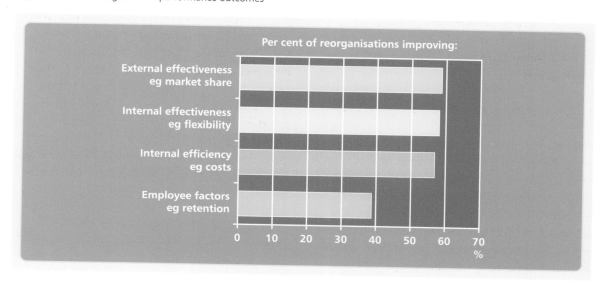

Figure 2 | Seven steps to successful reorganising

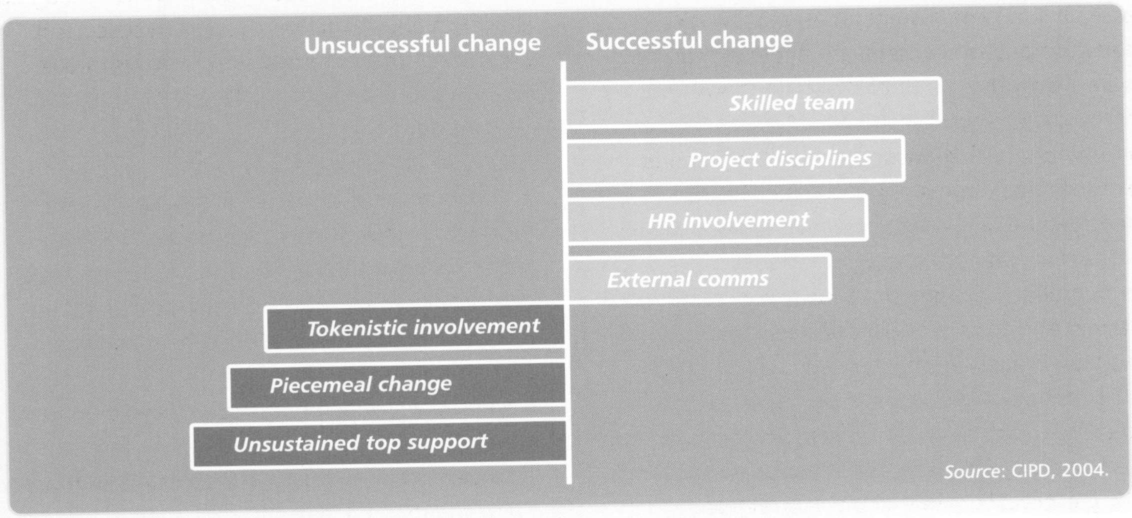

On the other hand, the 'seven steps' identify four kinds of action that more successful reorganisations typically emphasise heavily:

- effective external communications;
- involving HR in change management;
- maintaining good project management disciplines;
- having a skilled change management team.

While these 'seven steps' are based on private sector performance, both our surveys and our cases suggest their relevance to the public and voluntary sectors as well. Accordingly, although this report will go further, these 'seven steps' will provide a central thread orientating our discussion of effective reorganisation practice in the chapters that follow. Effectively the 'seven steps' place HR professionals in a central role as shapers of change and equip them with key factors for success in the management of reorganisations.

Scope of reorganisations

The reorganisations that we address in this report go beyond narrowly defined structural changes. We consider other kinds of reorganisation initiatives, including information systems changes, governance changes and relocations. All these reorganisations required parallel changes in so-called 'soft' areas in order to make them work. Our reorganisations, therefore, typically involve a good deal of attention to cultural, behavioural and communications issues. As the HR director in one of our case studies told us:

Organisational change is about more than re-drawing the lines and the boxes.

> '... the very fact of repeated restructuring is being used as evidence of its futility. This is a sceptical view we do not share.'

This does not mean that 'the lines and the boxes' of organisational charts are unimportant. Structural changes can be of great strategic significance, with widespread ramifications. Two examples from early 2005 illustrate this. At the beginning of this year, the Anglo-Dutch food and homecare giant, Unilever, announced a reorganisation that collapsed its old matrix structure into a simpler regional and key product area design. This structural change was strategically important, both to speed up decision-making and to increase responsiveness to consumer needs. American chip-making giant, Intel, likewise highlighted the strategic value of customer-responsiveness when it reorganised from three large technology-based groups into five smaller units focused on markets, such as corporate computing, digital homes and mobile computing. The ramifications of this touched directly on the HR agenda, as the new market-facing teams brought about a radical change in reward policy, moving from an individual to a collective focus.

Yet some experts now treat 'hard' aspects of organisation, such as structure, as increasingly irrelevant in today's complex, fast-moving and knowledge-intensive environment. From this point of view, 'the frequency with which organisations restructure themselves implicitly acknowledges that restructuring benefits have been hard to achieve or fleeting when achieved' (Oxman and Smith, 2003: 78). Here, the very fact of repeated restructuring is being used as evidence of its futility. This is a sceptical view we do not share.

To claim that the constant change in contemporary organisational structures demonstrates the inadequacy of structural solutions is to miss the point. It is the same logic as saying that the creation of new products and services in response to changing customer needs is an admission of failure. On the contrary, increasing the rate of change in products, services *and* organisation is a condition for success. Organisational structures have shorter life-cycles today, just as products and services do.

The reorganisations we report on here, therefore, typically have structural change close to their heart. Following Harold Leavitt (2003), we take organisational structures as an essential, if incomplete, tool in contemporary management.

Given the enduring importance of organisational structure, the critical issue is to make the structural tool work well. In today's conditions, this involves not a static, but a dynamic approach, a movement from structure to structuring, from organisation to organising. People issues are bound to be central to any such dynamic approach.

Background to the research

This is the final report from the 'Organising for Success' study, a three-year programme commissioned by the CIPD in 2002. It is based at the Saïd Business School, University of Oxford, but additionally involves researchers at the University of Edinburgh, the University of Reading and the Open University: Michael Mayer, Evelyn Fenton and Ann Smith, respectively. A high-level steering group of senior practitioners and experts has guided the research from the outset: steering group members are listed in the Acknowledgements.

The focus of the research has been on the 'how to' of reorganising. Given the constant flux of contemporary organisations, the practical issues of managing reorganisations have become more important than seeking after new 'cure-all' forms

'**Establishing effective practice in the detailed tasks and skills of getting reorganisations done is more pressing than outlining broad processes of organisational change.**'

of organisational structure such as network or modular forms. Establishing effective practice in the detailed tasks and skills of getting reorganisations done is more pressing than outlining broad processes of organisational change.

The starting point for the research was a scoping literature review, *Organising for success in the 21st century: a starting point for change* (Whittington and Mayer, 2002). Subsequent empirical research took two main forms, two mail surveys and longitudinal comparative case studies of reorganisation initiatives. Full details are available in the respective research reports, but a broad outline of methods is provided here.

The surveys

The research involved two surveys. The surveys were designed in close collaboration with senior HR professionals in our steering group and outside, supported by interviews and field-testing. Both surveys covered public, voluntary and private sector organisations, as well as managerial respondents from outside HR.

▫ *Survey One* was carried out in early 2003 to provide an initial overview of the field. This survey obtained a total of 881 usable responses, 62 per cent from HR professionals and 38 per cent from chief executive officers, split roughly evenly between the private sector and public and voluntary sectors. Full results from this survey are available in CIPD (2003), *Reorganising for Success: CEOs' and HR managers' perceptions.*

▫ *Survey Two* was carried out in mid-2004 and focused more on the skills, tools and competencies involved in reorganisations, the

ways in which managers learned to perform reorganisations and the role of HR professionals in these reorganisations. This survey obtained a total of 594 usable responses, with senior HR managers accounting for 38 per cent of the responses, and the remainder split between chief executives and senior finance, operations and IT managers. The public and voluntary sectors accounted for 63 per cent of the responses, while 37 per cent were from the private sector. Full results from this survey are available in CIPD (2004), *Reorganising for success: a survey of HR's role in change*.

The case studies

The research has also included 11 case studies of various types of reorganisations in different kinds of organisations (see Table 1 on page 6 for a summary). We deliberately included a wide range of sizes and sectors, in order to extend our ability to generalise our findings. At the same time, we sought some comparability through a policy of pairing: thus, we included two multinationals, two charities, two retailers, two organisations moving from public to private sectors and two local authorities.

We have tracked reorganisation initiatives from as early in the process as we could. Typically, therefore, we have been able to follow these reorganisations through more or less the whole process of implementation. Sometimes we have been involved from close to the design stage. The research included 134 formal interviews, over 100 of which have been tape-recorded, together with many more informal discussions and meetings. Interviews have been primarily with members of reorganisation teams, but also with chief executives, chairpersons and other senior

Table 1 | The 'Organising for Success' case studies

Case study	Type of organisation	Type of reorganisation	Research entry point	No. of employees
Cadbury Schweppes	Multi-national FMCG	Global IT implementation and culture change. Centralisation of shared services. Regional phased rollouts of customised business processes.	30 months into 60-month programme.	50,000
Lever Fabergé	Multi-national FMCG	Business unit integration of formerly separate home products and skin care companies, followed by culture change.	Second stage of 36-month 'continuous change' programme.	12,000
Major retail organisation	Retailer	Moving head office to new premises, complete departmental restructuring, and organisation-wide culture change.	One month after launch of 36-month project.	30,000
United Utilities	Utility company	Post-privatisation merger of electricity, gas and water utilities with very different organisational cultures.	Merger complete. 18 months into 24-month culture change.	25,000
Ordnance Survey	Digital geographical information provider	Public sector body moving towards a competitive commercial model, involving organisation-wide culture change and departmental restructuring.	20 months into 36-month programme.	5,000
United Bristol Healthcare Trust	Healthcare provider	Rationalisation of services traditionally provided by two different hospital trusts, including construction and relocation of facilities.	12 months into 60-month programme.	7,000

Case study	Type of organisation	Type of reorganisation	Research entry point	No. of employees
Nationwide	Retail bank	Business process engineering of Membership Account Administration, leading to centralisation of many administrative processes.	12 months into 36-month project.	16,000
National Open College Network	Qualifications accreditation network	From diverse network of volunteers, governed by committee, to private company with executive and board structure. Centralisation and coordination of administrative functions.	Beginning of 24-month project.	1,000 (network)
CACHE	Qualifications accreditation charity	From charitable sole provider of qualifications to childcare workers to provider competing with large industry rivals. Involved IT implementation, departmental restructuring and organisation-wide culture change.	At 'go live' in 24-month programme of work.	100
Northamptonshire County Council	Local government	IT-facilitated, comprehensive review and restructure of directorates to improve children's service delivery. IT-enabled move to e-government.	One month before 'go live' of 24-month programme.	20,000
Lewisham Borough Council	Local government	Comprehensive restructure of child welfare service directorate, involving management de-layering and appointment of new senior management team.	At initiation through to 'go live' – 12 months.	5,000

> **'The guiding proposition of this research is that reorganisation is a central concern for HR management.'**

managers to whom these teams reported. In addition, we typically have had access to internal documentation and we have sometimes observed critical events such as workshops and employee consultations. In five cases – Cadbury Schweppes, CACHE, Lever Fabergé, Lewisham Borough Council and the Ordnance Survey – we participated in joint research-in-action workshops bringing together the researchers, the case organisations and members of the research programme steering committee. Key findings from the case studies are presented in the report, *HR: Making change happen* (Molloy and Whittington, 2004).

Overall, the research design has emphasised multiple methods – surveys, cases and workshops. It has also drawn on multiple sources of experience – public, private and voluntary sectors, HR managers and other managers, large and small organisations. The research has been longitudinal, tracking reorganisations as they evolve, rather than looking back only in retrospect. All this increases the robustness of our findings and our confidence in their relevance beyond the particular contexts that we have studied.

Indeed, a key finding from our research across so many sectors and organisations is that certain good practices hold across widely different types of organisation. This is not to propose particular 'best practices' as universal and immutable prescriptions. Rather, there is a common repertoire of useful practices that are widely relevant but which have always to be applied selectively and adapted sensitively according to the needs of particular contexts. Mastering this common repertoire, and being able to use it discerningly, is critical to the effective management of

reorganisations in both private and public sectors, in large and relatively small organisations alike.

HR: shapers, not sweepers

The guiding proposition of this research is that reorganisation is a central concern for HR management. Reorganisations raise issues both in the technical specialisms of HR and the strategic domains (Miranda, 2005). There is clearly a substantial agenda in the functional core, as HR professionals deal with the implications of change, in terms of recruitment, redundancy, redeployment and training, just for example. But there is also a more strategic agenda, as HR has to engage directly in building the capabilities for change in the organisation and participate in shaping a change agenda that extends far beyond its heartland. This is a double challenge, because the two are interdependent. As we shall return to in Chapter 4, reorganisation inevitably raises strategic issues, but difficulties in the traditional core of HR work can easily derail the whole strategy.

A consequence of this double challenge is the need for HR professionals to engage in shaping reorganisations right from the design stage. HR must avoid the reactive position of picking up the pieces after reorganisations have happened. The predicament of the public sector HR manager quoted below, is to be avoided. Better by far is the position of the second manager, addressing the people agenda throughout. HR managers will be inescapably involved in change at some point, and they can be most effective in shaping reorganisations from the outset, rather than sweeping up afterwards. As we shall explore, this will require new attitudes and skill-sets amongst HR managers, from the detailed processes of project management to a confident understanding of overall strategy.

Sweeper or shaper?

More often than not, they [reorganisation teams] will come to us once they've decided what they want to do and need some assistance, which may mean advertising and developing job descriptions and, in the worst-case scenario, implementing redundancies.

HR manager, public sector (second research survey)

My roles in the project were multiple. [They were] to make sure that the people agenda was addressed throughout. To make sure that a balance was struck between ruthless efficiency and the needs of the people.

HR manager, United Utilities

These kinds of skill-sets and learning need to be developed among managers generally. The move to a hypercompetitive environment in the private sector (D'Aveni and Thomas, 2005), and the continuous change of the public sector, imply a significant extension to traditional managerial skills. The traditional approach required skill in managing the strategy, the product and the organisation. In a world of rapid change, however, the managerial task shifts from managing such static entities to coping with dynamic processes (Whittington, 2004). Managers will have to learn to cope with repeated strategising rather than fixed strategies; with innovating rather than the product management; organising rather than the organisation.

This shift towards dynamic processes involves a transformation of the managerial role, and the

skills required of it. Managers become regular strategists, innovators and organisers. These roles are highly demanding, involving change and uncertainty. Part of the strategic challenge for HR is to engage with and promote this shift, and we suggest that many of the skills and capabilities required for organising are likely to be typical for strategising and innovating more generally.

Summary

The pace of change is accelerating and reorganisations are an inescapable part of the managerial role. They are not to be ignored or disparaged, but accepted as an essential tool in organisational strategy. This Report documents contemporary practices in managing reorganisations, drawn from a wide range of sectors and organisations. The breadth of the experience reported here suggests that these practices will be relevant across many situations.

This chapter identified 'seven steps' towards successful organising, drawn from the experience of a large and diverse set of organisations. They will not work for every organisation in every circumstance, but together they pose a challenging checklist for anybody to consider before embarking on change. The following chapters explore these seven steps, and other important issues, in more detail, and close with a discussion of implications for the HR profession as a whole.

◻ Chapter 2 addresses the management of reorganisations, stressing particularly the importance of sustained top management support, the integration of reorganisation initiatives with broader changes and the role of effective project management.

- Chapter 3 focuses on teamwork in reorganisations, and the kinds of experience required by teams and the potential contribution of HR professionals to these teams.

- Chapter 4 turns to employees, the importance of communications and involvement and the dangers of tokenistic consultation.

- Chapter 5 returns to the relentless pace of reorganising, and the opportunities thereby thrown up for improving the skills and capabilities required for carrying reorganisations out more effectively.

- Chapter 6 summarises good practices in reorganisations and draws out implications for developing more successful reorganisation practitioners.

The overarching theme of the Report will be that HR professionals are inescapably becoming reorganisation practitioners. HR needs to be ready to step up to the challenge, and become shapers of reorganisations, rather than sweeping up afterwards.

2 | Managing reorganisations

◘ Reorganisations need consistent commitment from top management, secured by close identification with the organisation's strategic agenda.

◘ Reorganisations need to be aligned carefully with parallel changes in the organisation's business.

◘ Reorganisations require confident and flexible project and programme management skills.

Introduction

Reorganisations are expensive and complex activities. This kind of organising needs organising itself (Molloy and Whittington, 2005). As we shall see in this chapter, effective reorganisations need to secure top management support by demonstrating a clear contribution to strategic needs, manage implications for parallel changes in

the organisation and take a professional approach to project and programme management. Back-of-the-envelope charts and nimble improvisation are rarely enough. As one HR director told us, underlining the importance of an organised approach to organising:

It may be that some people can visualise what the new organisation should be, but they sure as hell cannot hold all the balls in the air to get them there.

Top management and the business case

Our largest case-study reorganisation, a global IT implementation project at Cadbury Schweppes, gives an indication of the resources, profile and timescales that can be involved in reorganisations. The project was scheduled over five years and, at its peak, involved 300 full-time dedicated staff, half of whom were external contractors. The Cadbury Schweppes chief executive at the start of

Figure 3 | Top management support and financial outcomes

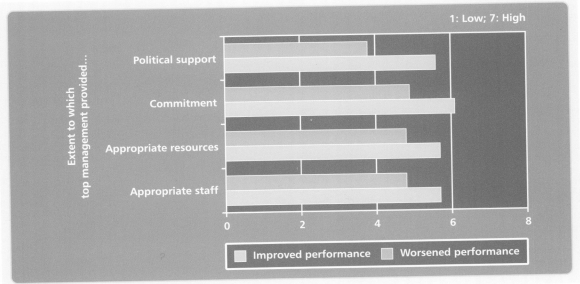

> **'Top management support can best be won by establishing a clear business case linked to the strategic needs of the business.'**

the project, John Sunderland (now Chairman), was personally identified with the project and financial analysts closely followed its progress. Reorganisations need top management commitment and a clear link to the strategy.

As the 'seven steps' introduced in Chapter 1 suggest, top management support is a critical condition for organising successfully. In particular, performance analysis of private-sector responses to our second survey shows that top managers' ability to demonstrate personal commitment and provide political support are two factors that discriminate substantially in terms of post-reorganisation financial outcomes (see Figure 3 on page 11). In those reorganisations where post-reorganisation performance worsened, political support and top management commitment were markedly lower than in reorganisations where post-reorganisation performance improved. Top management provision of staff and other resources were relatively unimportant in differentiating between successful and unsuccessful reorganisations. The message was similar in all our case studies, as exemplified by the following quotations from the Cadbury Schweppes and the Ordnance Survey case studies.

Top management commitment

The fundamentals are you need to have a really clear leader of the structure, somebody who has a very clear vision about what the endgame looks like.

Senior HR manager, Ordnance Survey

Senior management buy-in is absolutely fundamental for the process to work. ...There must be a vision, there must be a strategy and there must be support behind that.

Senior change manager, Cadbury Schweppes

Top management support cannot just be assumed. Our first survey found that, in one-quarter of reorganisations, the attitudes and behaviours of senior management had been significant constraints on success (CIPD, 2003). Commitment takes careful building and sometimes testing. As at Nationwide (see Case study 1, on page 13), this process of commitment building can easily be as much as six months long. In Ordnance Survey's reorganisation, there was a similar six-month period of engagement that started with the Board and cascaded down to the tiers of management immediately below. The test came with what was called the 'Ordnance Survey Experience', a major event inviting all employees to the Southampton headquarters. Personal commitment was demonstrated by the change team deliberately insisting that the 'Experience' should be hosted and fronted by senior management (Hutchinson, 2005).

Top management support can best be won by establishing a clear business case linked to the strategic needs of the business. From our first survey, we found that reorganisations were typically not directed simply at internal issues, but prioritised external objectives such as improving customer responsiveness, increasing market share and value for money (CIPD, 2003). As the senior manager from Lever Fabergé quoted below indicates, the case for the reorganisation should be fundamentally rooted in the needs of the business. Then, as reinforced by the second quotation, this purpose needs to be communicated with clarity and commitment.

Clarity of objectives

The essentials are around being absolutely clear about what it is you are trying to achieve and why – and I don't just mean the reorganisation. I mean: why are you even beginning to think about reorganising? Where do you want to be as a business?

Senior Manager, Lever Fabergé

Consistency of message and purpose is one of the most important success factors in any change programme. Crystal-clear purpose, understood by all, including 'what it means for me', should be made explicit.

Respondent to second survey

The business case for reorganisations often links directly to overall strategy. At Cadbury Schweppes, the vision was a global project 'PROBE' (Programme for the Realisation of Benefits from E-enabled Enterprise Resource Planning), designed to transform both the company's processes and people in order to achieve a step change in efficiency and sales growth. Similarly, the reorganisation we studied in a major retail organisation was part of a strategy to re-energise the brand in order to regain high street dominance. Moving headquarters from the traditional London offices was seen as an opportunity to support the vision of a 21st-century organisation worthy of a leading brand in tough high street retail space. At Ordnance Survey, the reorganisation agenda was at the heart of a transformation from a government provider of high-quality maps to a commercial provider of high-tech and high-specification digital geographical information to government, commercial and individual customers.

As the 'seven steps' indicate, however, top management support must be sustained beyond the initial business case and strategic rationale. The extended timescale involved in reorganisations inescapably means that change managers need to anticipate change in the change itself. Even the most rigorously managed projects may need to adapt. The five-year PROBE programme at Cadbury Schweppes metamorphosed into a more agile, flexible form in response to new business drivers, particularly a major new acquisition. In any extended change initiative, therefore, it seems that commitment is essential, but that the business case will need to be made and remade as the project proceeds.

Case study 1

Vision and the top at Nationwide

Nationwide has a standard formula for setting objectives and vision for change projects. It starts with an initial directive from the Board for change, then Nationwide Business Consultancy (NBC, the internal consultants) works out the vision, develops the business case and models the details of the processes. Ideas are typically held closely for at least six months, until accepted. The culture of Nationwide is to take organisational change slowly. The role of the sponsor of the reorganisation is very important in giving clear direction. A programme board is then set up underneath the sponsor to implement the vision.

Nationwide Business Consultancy typically goes through a four-stage process in any reorganisation:

1 Building the brief into a vision

For the Member Account Administration project (MAA), NBC developed the key notion of centralisation, indicating how it would tie into the low-cost, growth and diversifying strategies of Nationwide. This design work for MAA took around six months. Ideas for the project came from different places: internally within the NBC team, conversations around the business, external networking, and external benchmarking.

2 Developing a series of options to be discussed with the programme sponsor

The MAA project included options such as improving processes in the branch, doing administration regionally or centrally, or automating processes completely; and included the performance consequences of each. The final recommendation was drafted in a paper that was sent to stakeholders *via* the sponsor. The vision was then 'sold' to relevant executive directors and taken through the required 'political hurdles'.

3 Establishing the component parts of the overall programme

This occurs once the executive has cleared the final recommendation and the views of different parts of the organisation are fed into the design. In order to convince sceptics, a lot of business analysis is conducted to demonstrate the benefits of the reorganisation in monetary terms. As NBC begins on the detailed planning of the reorganisation, it draws up overarching process maps which detail all the activities required to conduct its business differently. It then works with the IT department to put a high-level technology plan into place. More recently NBC worked with its colleagues in IT to convert its automated process maps into coding which would enable it to automate all the new processes required for the reorganisation.

4 Examining and breaking down the overall processes

Each of the overall processes is then examined for the detailed processes involved and broken down into activities for implementation. For example, in the MAA project, opening an account or taking out a mortgage has its own process activity associated with it, which was redesigned in an optimum way. A team was set up to oversee Nationwide's process repository where all processes are documented to the same standard. These processes will be accessible for staff *via* the intranet with

the aim of getting a lot more control over processes within the business. For example, the procedures for filling in forms and the number of people involved with it are all documented *via* capacity and simulation modelling, to create an enterprise model for Nationwide. This will essentially become a blueprint for how Nationwide operates.

Managing interconnected change

Reorganisations should be closely aligned with the strategy and the rest of the organisation. As at Nationwide (see Case study 1), where technology and systems had already been changed, it is essential that the reorganisation should both have in place the necessary conditions for change and move in line with them. Any particular change relies upon 'complementary', or reinforcing, changes elsewhere in the organisation (Pettigrew and Whittington, 2001). As in the 'seven steps', piecemeal, uncoordinated change tends to lead to confusion and failure.

Reorganisations typically run parallel with other changes in the organisation. Our second research survey established that, in half the cases, reorganisations are closely connected to simultaneous changes in business processes, with parallel changes in information, accounting and control systems important in more than one-third of cases (CIPD, 2004). Specifically within the HR domain, reorganisations are heavily associated with concurrent changes in organisational culture and leadership style. Unfortunately, changes in 'harder' aspects of HR management, such as reward and career systems, are often given less emphasis.

Aligning reorganisation initiatives with these parallel changes in a complementary and

'Analysis ... shows that reorganisations which led to improved financial performance were also associated with greater emphasis on parallel changes in accounting and control systems and business processes.'

reinforcing fashion is important for financial outcomes. Analysis of our second survey data shows that reorganisations which led to improved financial performance were also associated with greater emphasis on parallel changes in accounting and control systems and business processes (see Figure 4, below). As we shall see in Chapter 5, many managers felt that HR system changes need greater attention in reorganisations.

Reorganisations and parallel changes typically follow substantial strategic and top management change. In the 12 months prior to their reorganisations, about half of the private-sector organisations in the first research survey had experienced significant changes in their markets, or products and services, or merger, acquisition or divestment activity (CIPD, 2003). A similar proportion had appointed a new chief executive in the previous year.

New chief executive appointments play a similar role in the public sector, with both the National Open College Network and Ordnance Survey specifically bringing in outsider chief executives as intended change agents. But here, the biggest precursor of reorganisation is increased collaboration with other agencies. At United Bristol Health Trust, for instance, reorganisation was driven in part by changes at the Strategic Health Authority level and the consequent need to collaborate directly with a host of private-sector contractors.

In other words, reorganisations are likely to be taking place within fast-moving contexts. This has implications for both project and programme management: projects will need some flexibility, and reorganisations will need integration within a fluid programme of parallel initiatives.

Figure 4 | Parallel change and financial outcomes

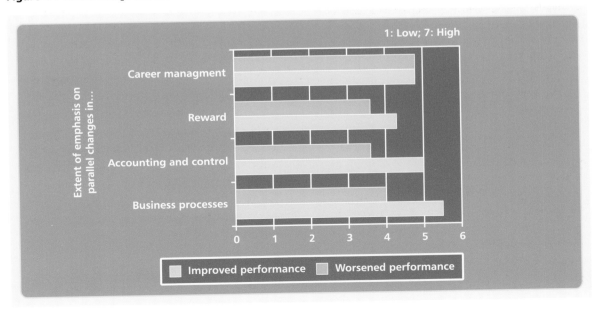

'Project management techniques are already very widely used in reorganisation initiatives.'

Project and programme management

The interconnection of reorganisation initiatives with other changes implies the importance of careful project management within a programme of parallel projects. The Nationwide four-step process shown in Case study 1, provides a classic model of converting a brief into a precise programme of change. Here, the change in perceptions required of the organisation necessitated a staged approach to implementation as the MAA project developed. The head of the Nationwide overall change programme stressed that MAA had to happen without turning the organisation upside down: business could not be put on hold while change was being implemented. MAA was slotted carefully into just 12 months of the overall three-year programme.

Within the overall programme, successful

reorganisations are associated with effective project management. Project management techniques are already very widely used in reorganisation initiatives (CIPD, 2004). Four out of five reorganisations establish formal statements of reorganisation objectives and set out timescales and milestones. The only project management technique that is significantly neglected is formal review of reorganisation projects after the event: this is skipped in more than 40 per cent of reorganisations. This neglect of review relates to weaknesses in learning, a theme we will return to in Chapter 5.

As indicated by Figure 5, below, the use of project management techniques is associated with better performance outcomes. Project management is one of our 'seven steps' of successful organising. Reorganisations with improved subsequent performance give more emphasis to setting formal

Figure 5 | Project management and financial outcomes

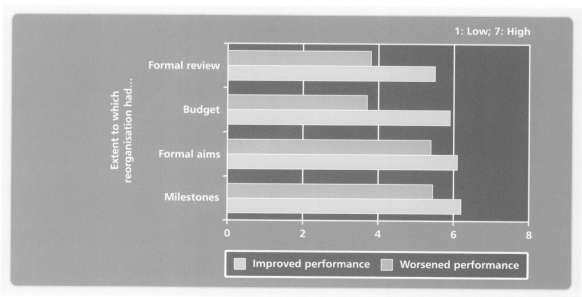

'**Reorganisations with improved subsequent performance give more emphasis to setting formal objectives, establishing milestones, budgeting and formal review.**'

objectives, establishing milestones, budgeting and formal review. Recalling the relative neglect of formal reviews, this is one area of project management in which organisations should clearly invest more.

Leading consulting companies routinely offer project and programme management services. In the public sector, projects are often managed using the PRINCE (Projects in Controlled Environments) methodology, now in its second generation. Standard software packages such as Microsoft Project, are also readily available. However, more than half the respondents to the second survey reported deficiencies in project management skills within the reorganisation team (CIPD, 2004). These skills are clearly something for organisations to develop.

However, some respondents and several of the case studies indicated limits to formal project management. First, project management can easily become mechanical and inflexible. As one respondent to the second survey warned:

Don't expect everything to work without some adjustment and don't be afraid to review changes at an early stage to keep the reorganisation on track.

Second, project management is itself a costly and time-consuming process that needs to be adequately budgeted for within the overall reorganisation process. In one of our cases, a senior manager observed how

…this great big machine called project planning comes in and it takes up vast amounts of time and systems space, because of all these critical paths which chunter away. Actually this is too big right now, and frightening people.

In this case study, the project management process got slimmed down halfway through.

Third, project management is liable to embed a sense of episodic, formalised change. The long-term process of integrating the two component companies of Lever Fabergé made much less use of project management than most of our cases, because senior management believed in the integration as a continuous journey rather than a set of discrete hurdles to be jumped. While some aspects of the integration of Lever Brothers and Elida Fabergé, such as financial systems, infrastructure and governance structures, were tightly project-managed, uniting the cultures of the two organisations to create a new Lever Fabergé culture was managed quite differently. The leadership team recognised that culture change could not be managed to specific deadlines, or directed at easily measurable targets and milestones. Culture change was facilitated instead *via* a series of engagement activities that were designed to enrol different people in different ways in a cumulative, rather than staged, fashion.

It is important, therefore, both to vest enough authority and experience in the project team in order to allow some appropriate relaxation of project disciplines, and to create sufficient trust and communications with the project sponsors for them to trust in the project's evolution. It is also important not to assume that good project management is all that is required, and to be aware when a less formalised and episodic approach may be more effective. Project management is not a cure-all.

'Projects will often need flexibility in implementation, objectives can shift and top management support needs constantly to be reaffirmed.'

Case study 2

Project management in the NHS

Reorganisation in the National Health Service is always a potentially politically-charged issue. The requirement for managing resources efficiently within strict financial controls and pressing demands from patients, clinicians and other medical practitioners is imperative. Further, NHS managers face intense scrutiny from the public and politicians and, therefore, need to be able to demonstrate transparency and accountability for their decisions and actions.

Under these conditions, project management is an essential tool in the NHS manager's repertoire. Many senior managers in the NHS are trained in the use of the PRINCE2 methodologies and regularly update their knowledge of this system as it evolves. Indeed, competency in the various levels of PRINCE2 can sometimes be a specific requirement of management appointments.

The benefits of PRINCE2 derive from the fact that it is a structured method providing the NHS with a standard approach to the management of projects. The method embodies proven and established best practice in project management. It is widely recognised and understood, providing a common language for all participants in the project.

Using the PRINCE2 methodology enables projects to have:

- A controlled and organised start, middle and end.

- Regular reviews of progress against objectives and against the business case.

- Flexible decision points.

- Automatic management control of changes to the project.

- Involvement of stakeholders and management at key phases

- Improved communication channels between the project, project management, and the wider organisation

For more information, visit the PRINCE website: www.ogc.gov.uk/prince2.

Summary

Reorganisations have to be organised too. They often involve substantial resources over extended periods of time. They will typically run parallel to other changes, and need careful alignment. The ordinary business of the organisation will need to be accomplished alongside: people have to carry out their day-to-day jobs as well as managing change.

The evidence from both surveys and case studies suggests some widely applicable good practices in managing reorganisations. Reorganisations should start with clear business objectives. They need consistent top management support. They benefit from rigorous project management, recognising the likelihood of parallel and interconnected change. None of these should be assumed as fixed, however. Projects will often need flexibility in implementation, objectives can shift and top management support needs constantly to be reaffirmed. Almost by definition, reorganisations take place in changing contexts.

3 | Teamwork in reorganisations

◘ It is important to invest in a strong reorganisation team, with the appropriate people, well-bonded together.

◘ Team skills for reorganisations are often best built in-house and can offer a good platform for future senior managers.

◘ HR professionals play a critical role in effective reorganisations, either directly, or in advisory roles.

Introduction

The last chapter highlighted various kinds of good practice in managing reorganisations. This chapter shifts the focus towards the kinds of managers and skills required for leading reorganisations. It starts by affirming the team nature of most reorganisation exercises and the consequent importance of care in both team selection and team building. It continues by identifying the critical roles HR professionals play in reorganisation teams and the positive outcomes associated with their involvement. Finally, the chapter considers the key skills and experiences typically required by reorganisation team members, and some implications for training and development.

The reorganisation team

Establishing the right project team for planning and managing reorganisations is critical. The project team will have to plan and manage the reorganisation. It will provide an on-going focal point for change. The team will act as a vanguard for ensuring change is accepted and implemented by the rest of the organisation. Ultimately, the team should be accountable for the success of the reorganisation project.

Getting the right team starts with selecting appropriate people. As one change programme director commented to us:

As long as you have the right people on the team, then the results will follow. That's why I spend a lot of time on choosing the team, with people that will work together.

The characteristics of the right team depend partly on the type of reorganisation that is being undertaken. We have found that relatively short, structural or infrastructural reorganisations, such as departmental reorganisations, require high degrees of internal knowledge and constrain the time available to search for and engage external consultants. In these cases, the team can typically be sourced internally. Longer-term projects, such as culture change programmes, long-term business process or IT systems restructuring that may take several years, often need much more external support. Table 2 (on page 20) summarises some of these considerations.

However, even with the right team members in terms of individuals, they will need bonding together. The team is likely to be working closely together under pressure: in a phrase from one of our case studies 'a lot of late-delivered pizzas get consumed'. Good interpersonal relationships are critical. As the following case study illustrates, Lever Fabergé goes to considerable lengths to help make sure that teams work well together.

Table 2 | Selecting the right team

Factor	Internal predominance	External predominance
Timing	• Short timescale. • Change needs to be made quickly. • Insufficient time to recruit consultants.	• Long timescale. • Change seen as on-going. • Time to choose the right consultants.
Knowledge	• Extensive, detailed knowledge of the organisation critical.	• Fresh, outside perspectives needed.
Capability	• Internal capabilities for change management. • Staff can be seconded.	• Internal capability for culture change not present. • Aim to develop internal capability.
Stakeholder issues	• High-risk stakeholder issues. • Internal team has credibility and clout.	• Low-risk from stakeholder issues. • Organisation receptive to outside influences.

Source: Molloy and Whittington (2004).

Case study 3

Lever Fabergé: Gelling in the Arctic

At Lever Fabergé, senior management recognised that team-building for their major change programme needed to start at the top. This was a key motivation for a week-long senior management team trip to the Arctic. In between cross-country skiing, hiking and riding snowmobiles, the senior management team focused on who they were as individuals, defining how they wanted to work together and how to open communication channels throughout the organisation. Subsequently, a number of two-day workshops were conducted for the whole of the marketing and sales organisation (about 450 people) by the senior management team that had been to the Arctic. Participants at the workshops discussed improving relationships in the organisation, understanding individual motivation and what it means to be in 'playing to win' mode as opposed to 'avoiding losing'. The workshops were also used to introduce people to the concept of giving and receiving feedback.

A follow-up conference for all 450 of the workshop participants was then held at Center Parcs. The conference was participative, with lots of activities in small groups and a healthy splash of humour. Sitting in conference rooms, looking at PowerPoint presentations was not the order of the day. The point was to find out how the strategy for growth could be brought to life and then to get people to think about how it was actually going to be done.

> **'The experience of United Utilities and other case-study organisations affirms the value of developing in-house teams to manage reorganisations.'**

Since the company conference, the senior management team has had several more 'away-days' to formulate next steps and share experiences of what each other has been doing. There is a sense of momentum that needs to be built upon and kept going. In a tough sales environment, attention has increasingly turned to thinking about the communication from the chairman and the board on how to turn up the pressure in the organisation to really focus on results delivery. The right organisational style, organisational culture and leadership are regarded as being crucial to delivering hard business results. Consequently, communication from the top of the organisation has been empowering, direct and clear about what needs to be done, yet without being felt as 'a big whip on the business'. As a result, the organisation has felt inspired rather than stressed. The aim has been

…to get people close to the flames so that they feel the heat, but not so close that they go into a negative mind set.

Table 3 (on page 22) provides a breakdown of roles and responsibilities in reorganisation teams across our second survey sample. General managers, ie business or departmental heads, typically take the leadership roles. The interconnected nature of reorganisations, however, means that reorganisation teams need to draw on a wider range of expertise. Thus, finance, human resource and operations managers also take prominent roles. We will explore the part played by HR executives specifically, in the next section.

Reorganisations can be an excellent opportunity to develop managers. At United Utilities, the post-merger integration team was deliberately made up of high achievers with senior management potential. Almost all of these managers then went on to leading positions within the company. A senior HR manager commented on the role of this project in developing this group of managers thus:

To just have line experience on its own, I think is okay. But to have line experience and project experience, big change projects, I think is very important, because many big organisations will be almost constantly undergoing big change programmes, either a building move or a behavioural change or whatever it may be. It's very important to have that experience of understanding how projects work.

The transition from project roles back to senior line positions is not an automatic one, however. At one of our case-study organisations, some managers became trapped in a series of projects simply by virtue of their accumulating project management expertise. United Utilities had taken very deliberate steps to ensure a route back into line management. By clarifying the career path forward, United Utilities ensured a team that was both highly capable and highly motivated.

The experience of United Utilities and other case-study organisations affirms the value of developing in-house teams to manage reorganisations. As Table 3 shows, external consultants are typically not attributed influential roles. Nevertheless, all but one of our case-study reorganisations made use of external consultants, and the exception, Nationwide, had a well-established internal consultancy organisation. Consultants are easily disparaged, but not so easily done without.

External consultants can fulfil a wide range of functions, from assistance in the design of the reorganisation and knowledge of similar changes elsewhere, to the provision of specialist areas of expertise such as communications, or the supply of skilled facilitators to assist in large-scale implementation. At a major retail organisation, it was external consultants who managed almost all the detailed process of implementing the head

'There might be a reluctance to hand over significant influence to consultants …
but nonetheless, there are plenty of specialised roles that consultants can
productively take.'

Table 3 | Roles and representation in reorganisation teams

	Leadership role (%)	Major, but not leadership role (%)	Moderate role (%)	Minor role (%)	No role (%)
General manager	72	18	4	2	5
Internal HR	12	62	17	5	5
Internal consultant	5	15	9	8	62
Internal finance	15	36	26	11	11
Internal IS/IT	6	23	26	20	25
Internal operations	10	30	20	9	30
External consultant	5	22	11	13	48

Source: CIPD (2004), non-HR respondents only.

office move and introducing new ways of working at the same time. This involved a comprehensive and integrated understanding of the strategic needs of the business, HR systems and processes, IT systems, logistics, building regulations and people management issues. In many ways, consultants were much better-placed to overcome many of the challenges of this particular project, as they already had access to the specialised knowledge and experience gained elsewhere, freeing up the organisation to concentrate on delivering business as usual. There might be a reluctance to hand over significant influence to consultants, as indicated in Table 2, but nonetheless, there are plenty of specialised roles that consultants can productively take.

The ideal reorganisation team should include senior management, or at least ensure close liaison with them through regular and formal mechanisms. In larger organisations, reorganisation project teams typically report to some kind of formally constituted project steering or sponsoring group. Steering group membership is important here, too. Ideally, a chief executive or unit head, providing a clear symbol and direct

> **'While there are different ways of structuring large projects, the consistent message is that projects must have leadership and senior management buy-in.'**

reinforcement of top management commitment, heads these. For large and extended projects, such top-management involvement may shift over time, but at the start, at least, it is an important signal: in the Cadbury Schweppes PROBE project, the chief executive took a strong lead in the formative stages of the project, before gradually letting a board of 'process directors' drawn from senior management in the company take more of the leadership.

While there are different ways of structuring large projects, the consistent message is that projects must have leadership and senior management buy-in. Where senior management is not present directly in the governance of a project, as a director, for example, there must be clear, regular and consistent lines of communication, for example *via* a steering group or reporting schedule.

Case study 4

Enrolling senior managers at Ordnance Survey

Extensive, detailed work with the senior management team around defining a vision and strategy for Ordnance Survey, established a consensus that change was necessary. The next stage was to get that understanding out across the whole of the organisation. The consultants developed an event called 'The Ordnance Survey Experience', hosted at head office in the business centre (Hutchinson, 2005). All 2,000 Ordnance Survey employees attended the week-long, large, interactive engagement process. Participants arrived in groups every half-hour for a four-hour session, were handed a 'learning guide' and invited in to 'just have an experience'.

The experience consisted of a presentation from the deputy CEO on what Ordnance Survey was today. This was followed by a history of Ordnance Survey, how it

came about, how it had evolved and changed over the years and what some of the options might be for its continued growth and development. In addition to emphasising that Ordnance Survey had always been a dynamic organisation responding to and exploiting new technology, and that further change lay ahead, the experience was designed to get participants individually to answer four key questions:

◘ What is the Ordnance Survey vision?

◘ Why is the vision important to the business?

◘ What does that vision mean for me as an individual?

◘ What can I do to help the organisation to achieve it?

In order to enable people to answer these questions, each zone of the Ordnance Survey experience would have a challenge for them to complete, the answers to which were contained somewhere in the zone. Senior management, wearing green t-shirts to enhance visibility, were present throughout and available to discuss the experience with other participants. For some of the senior managers, this lack of formality took a little getting used to. However, in the words of a member of the senior management team:

There were all sorts of challenges for both the senior management team and the people. What this event really did was to move up the senior management in the eyes of the workforce. To help them understand that there was some skill and ability in our senior team and they were all committing to do things in a different way and to start leading the business more effectively.

Formal senior management involvement is critical for two reasons. First, the project team may need the legitimacy and authority of senior management to drive changes through. As at Ordnance Survey (Case study 4), senior

> 'Chief executive respondents ... rated HR specialists as the most important source of advice and learning with regard to the processes and methods of reorganisation.'

management must be clearly enrolled in the change. Second, the senior management team and leadership need a finely-tuned awareness of the progress of change projects, including the challenges they face, in order to be able to respond and adapt to issues before they develop into a crisis. Large-scale, high visibility projects that are seen to be out of control can damage reputations and be expensive to fix.

The role of HR managers

HR managers are taking prominent roles in reorganisations. As indicated by Table 3 on page 22, HR managers are seen by other executives as having a major project role in almost two-thirds of cases, and second only to finance specialists as the functional area most likely to be leading reorganisations. In a sense, this is not surprising: human resource issues are central to reorganisations. Reorganisations raise core HR

issues such as redundancies, relocations and reward, and many of our case-study managers emphasised the importance of getting these aspects of change right. As we shall describe in Chapter 4, core areas of HR activity should be working well if a more strategic and transformational role is to be performed successfully. An unfair dismissal or botched communication can derail the whole change process.

However, the HR function can, and does, play a more significant role than just smoothing the process and sweeping up. Although chief executives or senior general managers typically lead the reorganisation, HR managers often exercise important influence. Chief executive respondents to the second survey rated HR specialists as the most important source of advice and learning with regard to the processes and methods of reorganisation. Finance and operations specialists come some way behind (see Figure 6).

Figure 6 | Functional sources of useful learning

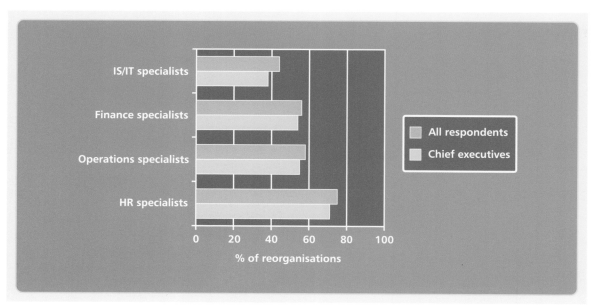

Moreover, HR staff input, promoting the people agenda, is adding significant value. Our first research survey established that where human resource managers are involved in steering groups or reorganisation project management teams, reorganisations perform significantly higher across a range of variables, from internal and external effectiveness, to increased efficiency and especially better employee-related factors, such as morale and key staff retention (see Figure 7, below). These relationships hold even excluding responses from HR professionals (CIPD, 2003). Having HR professionals closely involved in the reorganisation team and process is another of our 'seven steps' to successful organising.

HR professionals should not take their involvement for granted, though. One respondent to our first survey exclaimed: 'in my case…very little input was permitted from me, and I headed the HR function!' A place in the reorganisation team has to be earned, and it takes the right skills and capabilities to ensure inclusion and impact.

Skills and capabilities

The case-study quotations below indicate how easy it is to talk about change, but how important it is to be able to actually 'walk that talk'. Reorganisation teams often lack the required experience and skills. Chapter 2 pointed to the importance of skills in project management, in making a business case rooted in strategy, in managing links with senior management and in keeping aligned with parallel changes. This section introduces another set of skills – people management skills – which we will describe further in the next chapter, too.

Figure 7 | HR staff impact on reorganisation outcomes

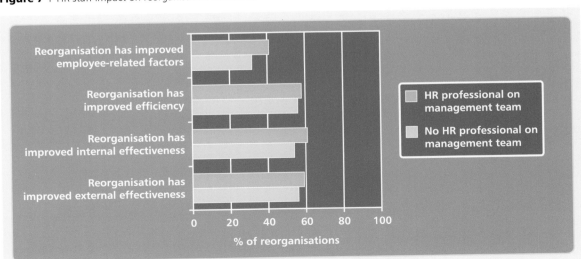

> **'Projects with a high information technology content can be particularly liable to neglect people management and communications skills.'**

Only talk

In this sector, many managers are very proficient at talking about change management but lack the experience and confidence to do it.

Respondent to second survey

And the top leadership have to 'walk the talk'. At the end of the day, I think people watch your feet, not your lips.

Senior manager, Lever Fabergé

Indeed, our second survey identified skills in people management as the most important enabler of success in reorganisation teams (see Figure 8,

below). Projects with a high information technology content can be particularly liable to neglect people management and communications skills. In one of our case studies, a senior HR manager commented:

The danger was that our project managers – very good at the nuts and bolts stuff – managed the projects but ignored some of the 'softer' issues. As HR, we built in a dedicated people stream for the appointments activity and the communications activity. Changing the organisation systems and processes has to be done alongside addressing the people issues of the transition.

HR managers become guardians and guarantors of the people agenda in reorganisations.

Figure 8 | Team skills and financial outcomes

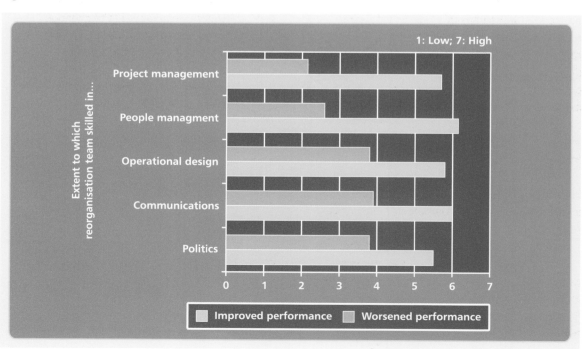

'... what counts is the ability to identify the unique issues in each situation and to be able to draw upon generic skills, tools and techniques to deal with them.'

Nevertheless, Figure 8 does emphasise the range of skills successful reorganisation teams should have: people management and project management are at the top, but skills in organisation design, communications and organisational politics are substantial differentiators between success and failure. This range of reorganisation skills is not easily built up.

Of course, a team can cover this range by selecting individuals with particular strengths. Yet many of our reorganisation managers had developed this breadth of skills for themselves. Many had done MBAs or other postgraduate management degrees. Some learnt from participating in specialised professional networks, such as the United Kingdom branch of the Organization Design Forum (www.organizationdesignforum.org) and various CIPD forums (www.cipd.co.uk/communities). The most common denominator, however, was the wide range of organisational experience successful change practitioners had developed. Sometimes this was *via* employment in consulting firms; often it was the product of careers pursued across different organisations and different sectors. The fact that these diverse experiences could be relevant across a range of contexts reinforces our point from Chapter 1 on the commonality of the basic good practices in reorganisations and the opportunity of learning from the experiences of others.

Thus, many of our most seasoned reorganisation leaders had built up a wide range of experiences through direct employment in a number of different organisations across different sectors. At CACHE, the deputy CEO and HR Director were taken on precisely because of their experience of change management in borough councils and the hotel industry, respectively. In Cadbury Schweppes, most of the change management leaders had

experience of other organisations and sectors. At Ordnance Survey, change management and organisational development leaders were brought in from sectors as diverse as banking, retail and beverages. Such change leaders, even with HR functional backgrounds, were often reluctant to identify themselves as simply HR professionals, and many had deliberately acquired experience in other roles.

What these individuals share are the requisite generic skills – especially in project management – and an informed overview of the people, process and technology issues encountered in change programmes. Of course, each organisation and every project will have important differences: what counts is the ability to identify the unique issues in each situation and to be able to draw upon generic skills, tools and techniques to deal with them.

Given the relevance of certain generic tools and skills, consultancy experience in the change management team can be a particularly useful resource. At United Utilities, there was little internal experience of running large change projects and the integration of the two merged companies was overdue. Part of the solution was to hire in change managers with consulting experience. As one ex-consultant at United Utilities put it:

So you take the [major consultancy] methodology cookbook and you apply things from it and other projects that I worked on, and you get a really nice strong sense of the right way to do things.

Change management experience can be plugged in, but needs to be adapted.

At Cadbury Schweppes, experience in change management is highly valued and something they actively seek to recruit into the organisation. The following case study shows the job specification for a Cadbury Schweppes change integration manager, illustrating the range of experience and skills they are typically looking for.

Case study 5

Profile of a Cadbury Schweppes change integration manager

1 Purpose

Contributing to enabling the realisation of benefits via a change strategy that includes the establishment of new ways of working, job and organisation design, training, stakeholder engagement and communications.

2 Accountabilities

Providing thought leadership, coaching, challenge and facilitation in the following areas:

a) *Ensuring organisational design supports the change agenda by*

- identifying the change impact of new processes and systems

- incorporating job design principles into local job design

- ensuring performance measures reflect line of sight between individual performance and business goals

- capturing and redefining 'Policies and Procedures' which reinforce new processes and ways of working

- orchestrating role and relationship mapping, ensuring clarity across processes.

b) *Developing the change agenda by*

- championing development of a strong team culture through cross-process integration

- coaching project team managers to act as role models

- translating organisation concepts into practical business solutions, supporting leadership team to embed new ways of working and behaviours

- ensuring 'change readiness' within the business and developing transition plans

- sharing project experience learning with colleagues at the centre and other BUs.

c) *Stakeholder management and communications*

- facilitating building commitment for the organisation change requirements

- developing a communications strategy and plan

- monitoring and reviewing effectiveness of communications and stakeholder management.

d) *Training and education*

- orchestrating the education and training strategy to ensure user and other employees are clear on their roles and ways of working, and have the necessary capability to perform their jobs

- ensuring appropriate level of competence by post-training assessments and remedial training for systems users

- ensuring interventions such as STC and new ways of working are adapted and highly targeted to specific team requirements.

> 'The message…is that the skills and capabilities of change management are challenging and diverse.'

e) *Developing and maintaining the overall capability of project team members throughout the project lifecycle by*

◻ determining skill gaps of existing CS personnel, identifying any external resource requirements

◻ ensuring that knowledge is effectively transferred when people move in, across or out of the project

◻ acting as a coach, delivering and advising on performance and development issues, ensuring that performance management process is being followed and applied to CS and external resources.

f) *Effective project management*

3 Prerequisites

◻ Work experience and specialist knowledge in organisational development/design and change management (could include consulting background and/or extended experience in managing complex change projects).

◻ Coaching and facilitation skills.

◻ Consulting and contracting skills.

◻ Strategic understanding of business levers.

This Cadbury Schweppes change integration job specification exemplifies many of the themes of this chapter and preceding ones. It highlights the connection between change and business goals, and the importance of a strategic understanding of business levers. It underlines the role of team cultures within change projects. It identifies the importance of ensuring appropriate skills within change teams. It emphasises effective project management and experience of managing

complex change projects in the past. It recognises organisation design skills, but sees broader change management, coaching and facilitation skills as important as well. Consulting skills, and experience in dealing with consultants, are highlighted, too.

The message from the Cadbury Schweppes job specification, and one from this chapter overall, is that the skills and capabilities of change management are challenging and diverse. Some of these skills and capabilities are relatively easy to specify and identify; others are more subtle, involving personal style. As a Cadbury Schweppes change manager observed:

It's not just what you do but how you do it… Critical is the ability to collaborate and co-create, so that the solution is owned by the implementing unit or team. It involves large amounts of facilitation and having an antenna about what is going on.

Summary

This chapter has focused on the importance of the people leading reorganisations. They need to be selected carefully and then bonded together effectively. At some time, however, reorganisation teams will be disbanded and, as at United Utilities, careers need to be managed forward. HR managers often play a central role in these reorganisation teams, sometimes as project leaders, but often as important influencers, too. The skills and capabilities needed to win an influential place in reorganisation teams are not acquired easily: many of our reorganisation leaders had previously managed change in a diverse set of organisations beforehand.

A core capability identified in this chapter, however, is the importance of taking people management issues seriously. Skills in people management are rated as the most important skill in enabling reorganisations, and having HR professionals formally represented is associated with superior results. The management of employees in reorganisations is the central theme of Chapter 4.

4 | Employees in reorganisations

□ Do not assume employee resistance: employee support can be won, but must be worked for.

□ Good employee communications and consultation pay off, but need appropriate time and resources.

□ Do not neglect core HR issues: reorganisations involve a lot of conventional HR as well as strategy.

Introduction

People are at the heart of organisations. Getting them onboard, and keeping them there, is vital to the success of reorganisations. After all, as one of our service case study organisations reminded us: 'our employees are ambassadors for us; they need to be brought in'. Confusion on the part of market-facing employees, or worse antagonism, has a direct impact on customers. And, recalling Chapter 2, the first research survey indicated that employee-related outcomes were the most problematic of all in reorganisations.

Facing change

Reorganisations inevitably prompt anxiety amongst employees. Jobs, careers, skills, locations and much more are at stake. Even apparently trivial changes can easily rupture the kinds of informal relationships that make work worthwhile for many employees. Often, they threaten the psychological contract of mutual obligation between employees and employers on which superior performance relies. But resistance need not simply be assumed, and there are ways in which to manage it.

A good first step is to recognise that there is plenty of reason for anxiety. About half of the reorganisations represented in our second survey involved involuntary redundancies; 10 per cent involved involuntary redundancy for more than one-fifth of the workforce. On top of these, there are substantial voluntary redundancies, early retirements and job moves (CIPD, 2004).

Yet reorganisations are not necessarily simply negative. Two-thirds of reorganisations in the second survey involved some hiring and 85 per cent involved at least some retraining. Thus, even where there is redundancy, there is often hiring and upskilling. Moreover, respondents estimated that in two-thirds of reorganisations, employees were generally accepting of change. In other words, although reorganisations can be extremely disturbing, there is typically both some willingness and some 'up-side' upon which to build.

Managing reorganisations positively may involve challenging employees' memories of earlier ones. At one of our large organisations, an earlier takeover had left a bad impression. The reorganisation team emphatically managed things differently this time:

There was a legacy issue about the takeover, which was that all the senior people [from one company] got sacked. And it was all done in secret. So we consciously said that [as] part of the style of doing this project we will make the appointments 'in plain sight'. Everybody will see how people get appointed and we will deal properly with the casualties, whereas the other guys were just kneecapped and got rid of, they were literally given plastic bags with their stuff in and told to leave the premises. We consciously said we will not adopt that style here.

HR Director, case-study organisation

> **'Employee support should be monitored continuously and comprehensively throughout the change programme.'**

The reorganisation team invested heavily in communications, workshops and symbolic actions, including face-to-face meetings with the senior management team, to underline that this time the reorganisation would be done differently.

Even where reorganisations are being managed positively, employee support must be continuously worked on. At one organisation, an HR manager remembered that everything started as 'all positive, positive, positive; everyone was singing from the same hymn sheet'. But one small incident concerning the implementation of a new IT network caused latent resistance to surface and nearly derailed the whole change programme, not to mention the career of the manager responsible. Getting the details right is an important theme in the reorganisation cases we studied and an issue we shall return to in the final section of this chapter.

Employee support should be monitored continuously and comprehensively throughout the change programme. This monitoring can provide early warnings of counter-productive resistance, and timely signals of other problems that need responding to. At Nationwide, the internal consultancy group has developed a system of 'heat maps' to indicate the extent to which their various internal clients are 'hot' or 'cold', and to guide actions to restore support or fix problems. The underlying message is that employee support cannot be taken for granted and must be won and re-won continuously through the reorganisation. Our research shows that excellent communications and genuine consultation are critical tools for success in reorganisations.

Communications and consultation

Communications should be multi-directional (Whittington *et al*, 2005). As in Chapter 2, top management needs constantly to be kept informed. At the same time, communications should be managed carefully with external

Figure 9 | External communications and financial outcomes

stakeholders – customers, suppliers, shareholders and local communities. Indeed, external communications constitute one of our 'seven steps' of successful organising. As indicated by Figure 9, opposite, reorganisations that are financially more successful typically invest in substantially more external communications with suppliers, customers and financial stakeholders than do unsuccessful reorganisations.

Here, though, we shall concentrate on internal communications with employees. To start with, there are legal obligations. From April 2005, the new Information and Consultation of Employees Regulations require organisations with 150 or more employees to inform and consult employees on management decisions affecting their future, including changes in organisation of the work or the workforce, and changes relating to the financial situation, structure and employment of staff. But, legally required or not, our research found that communications and consultation in reorganisations are simply good practice anyway. Employees can become informed participants in change; the reorganisation team can anticipate and adjust to unforeseen problems. As in the quotations that follow, communications, consultation and involvement are vital to making reorganisations happen.

Making it happen

I learnt a massive amount about the need to communicate, communicate, communicate. That concept forms the grounding for all the organisational work I have done after that. The communication, consultation and involvement strategy is what will make it happen.

Change manager, public sector case study

Consult to death with management, staff and unions.

Respondent, second survey

In four out of five reorganisations, respondents to our second survey claimed to have explained the changes extensively to employees (CIPD, 2004). From our cases as well, newsletters, emails, intranets and workshops appear to be standard procedure. But often this sort of communication fails to engage, and too often it is only one-way and top-down. According to the second survey, one-third of reorganisations are not providing significant opportunities for basic feedback and questioning from employees, and nearly half admit to limited investment in the genuine consultation implied in the regulations (CIPD, 2004).

Multi-channel communications

There are a number of different intelligences that people have. So it is not just written communications. There are rhetorical, visual, practical, even musical ways in which people learn, which people have different preferences for. So, in passing on information, it is looking for different ways of getting that over to different intelligences that is critical to getting it taken on board.

Change manager, Ordnance Survey

Well, the lesson I learned was that you had to use every medium that was available to you and just exploit all the channels.

HR manager, United Utilities

Engaging with all employees will typically mean making use of all available channels. One

> **'Employee engagement means that communications must go beyond simple box ticking.'**

reorganisation communications programme had to be reviewed when it was realised that not only did a sizeable minority of employees not have access to email, but that some could not read or write. As in the earlier quotation from the Ordnance Survey, it is important that communications programmes recognise the different kinds of 'intelligences' that employees have. Many employees will not engage strongly with simple written formats.

Employee engagement means that communications must go beyond simple box ticking. Instead, we found that managers often had to put real imagination and passion into making their messages real. Face-to-face communications, especially from the leadership, were often critical: this became a strong feature at United Utilities, where the management style had traditionally been more remote (see Case study 6, below).

Techniques such as role-playing, encouraging people to enact different behaviours and positions of responsibility helped here, too, typically with the support of specialist trainers.

Case study 6

Getting people on board at United Utilities

At United Utilities every employee in the organisation attended a two-day away-day designed to introduce them to the new values and culture of the organisation and new ways of working. Every event was attended by at least one director or the chief executive. This involved 25,000 people over 18 months – a major project in itself. Starting with the top team, selected employees were trained to facilitate the away-days and cascade the same event throughout the organisation, training other employees in the process. This undertaking was a radical departure from the previous management style, not least because never before had the organisation carried out the same event for everyone in the organisation, whether they were chief executive or an operative. The key aim was to get everyone to work through actions and behaviours with their managers and work teams and to give feedback to each other in a constructive way. As the project manager pointed out, the unfamiliar approach produced some surprising results:

Sitting in a room in a semi-circle, no table, two facilitators and, you know, sort of sharing experiences. It's very alien to a lot of our people. There are people who go on the workshops who were cynics, completely, at the beginning, who are almost like it's a revelation about what they found out about themselves. You know, almost evangelic! Gets a bit scary.

At the end of the two-day workshop, people came away with a 'blue chip', a bit like a casino chip, that represented issues that were important to them as individuals. The idea behind this was that, in the event of the employee feeling that they were not being fully listened to, they could refer to the blue chip as a way of ensuring that their concerns would be acknowledged in a mutually supportive way. As a means of continuing to capture the learning from the workshops, each participant had a 'buddy' allocated to them, with whom they could meet up after the workshop, at any time. The value was summed up by the HR manager as follows:

So you go on the workshop. You have the two days and you come away with better understanding within the team. You come away, perhaps, with something that the team have said that they will do. And mostly you've had a chance to spend some time with people out of work that you wouldn't normally.

In other reorganisations, communications involved physical symbols and activity. Walking people

'...the big difference between successful and unsuccessful reorganisations was in the extent to which they invested in consultation and involvement.'

around a new building, showing them new office mock-ups, and pointing out even basic things like where the coffee machine will be, help employees to visualise and internalise how things will be in the new organisation. Physical symbols can often convey a lot more than simple words. At the Ordnance Survey, the transformation journey was mapped on to a carpet that employees could actually walk along. During the Ordnance Survey Experience, employees were invited physically to go through either of two doors, one indicating support of the changes, one indicating reservations.

Communications strategies could go even further and entail real involvement in decisions about the nature of the changes and/or their implementation. Unfortunately, this is not yet common. In our second survey, we found only 29 per cent of reorganisations claiming significant involvement of this kind (CIPD, 2004). And very few of our case studies made the kind of commitment to involvement attempted by CACHE, for instance (see Case study 7).

This kind of substantive involvement can make a substantial difference to financial outcomes. Reorganisations that led to superior financial outcomes invested little more in basic explanation and information than those that experienced inferior outcomes. As in Figure 10 (on page 36), the big difference between successful and unsuccessful reorganisations was in the extent to which they invested in consultation and involvement. Involvement in decisions about the nature and implementation of the reorganisation is one of our 'seven steps' to success.

Case study 7

Representation and consultation at CACHE

Direct face-to-face contact with senior management proved to be an effective method of reassuring employees that their interests and concerns were being sincerely listened to. At CACHE, a much smaller organisation with 100 employees, four elected representatives were chosen to participate in discussions with the senior management team. The role of the representatives was to act as a conduit for comments and information about the reorganisation process. These representatives had personal responsibility for keeping all staff updated with progress *via* e-mail. The representatives were trained for the role by specialist consultants along with members of the HR team. HR took minutes of the meetings between the representatives and senior management team and these were then circulated *via* e-mail to all staff. The meetings were held during normal working hours.

An innovative process was initiated in order to elect the representatives. First, nominations for representatives were requested by HR. Each person who stood for election needed two other members of the organisation to sign a memo in support. If more than four people were nominated, a ballot would be held with the winners being the first four past the post. In the event of a tie, the chief executive was to toss a coin in the presence of both nominees. In addition to the system of elected representatives, CACHE also placed a suggestion box at reception for staff who wished to contribute other ideas about the reorganisation, at any time. These regular meetings with employees, coupled with question-and-answer sheets, served to break down fears about job security and mistrust of management during the change process.

'**It is important to do communications and consultations properly, but this will require clear and substantial budgeting at the outset of the reorganisation project.'**

Figure 10 | The effect of employee involvement on financial outcomes

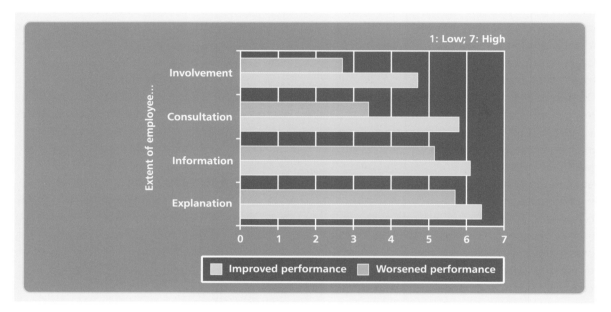

The kind of involvement and consultation described here needs to be sustained and genuine. In one reorganisation, employees had been thoroughly involved at the start, with options presented to them to discuss. However, as pressures mounted, the involvement process lapsed and the reorganisation leader admitted: 'people felt used'. In our first survey, 64 per cent of respondents said they would do more consultation in the next reorganisation they undertook (CIPD, 2003).

Even if our evidence suggests substantial benefits, the costs of effective communications and sustained and genuine involvement should not be underestimated. At Lever Fabergé, the change team identified 26 distinct audiences with whom they had to manage consistent communications. Northamptonshire County Council tested its vision and change principles with 77 groups before

'going live'. As we have seen from Case study 6, the away-day events at United Utilities involved 25,000 people. It is important to do communications and consultations properly, but this will require clear and substantial budgeting at the outset of the reorganisation project.

Getting core HR right

So far, many of the themes of this Report involve extending the HR function beyond its traditional specialisms: for example, aligning with strategy, participating in multi-functional change teams, and using change tools such as communications and project management. However, implementing reorganisations inescapably involves core HR issues ranging from recruitment and redundancy to employee relations, training and reward. It is the HR manager's job to ensure that these are recognised from the start and carried out well.

> 'Our case studies have emphasised the importance of making sure that core HR systems are roadworthy before setting out on the long and demanding journey of change.'

After all, as one of our case-study HR directors told us, 'reorganisations have finally to be populated with people'. Hitches in the detail can bring the whole reorganisation process grinding to a halt.

The detail can be overwhelming: reorganisations are likely to involve redundancies, recruitment, new job- and people-specifications, revised salary scales, competency models, training needs analyses, skills gap audits, coaching, union meetings and grievance procedures. This will require careful coordination within the HR function. In one of our cases, 'transactional HR' (concerned with payroll and similar) had been hived off to a separate building on an industrial estate far from headquarters, where 'transformational HR' was located. The reorganisation suffered glitches as the two sites struggled to coordinate, and deliberate efforts had to be made to restore the links between the two. It is dangerous to sideline the detail. Strategic HR does not operate in a different sphere from the tactical: they are mutually complementary.

The message from our cases is to prepare in advance and, fundamentally, to ensure that core HR policies are in place and functioning smoothly before starting out on the reorganisation. As a senior HR manager at Lewisham Borough Council insisted: 'the basic procedures need to be right – that's essential for credibility'. Reorganisations are long and testing journeys and HR will need a roadworthiness test and thorough service beforehand. Therefore, the skills of HR

professionals in employee communications, consultation and involvement can be utilised to have a major impact on the success of reorganisations.

Summary

Reorganisations are fundamentally about people and HR professionals are bound to be involved. A theme of this report has been that HR should be shaping reorganisations, rather than sweeping up after them. But a condition for being an effective shaper of change is that the essential details of the task need to be attended to as well. Our case studies have emphasised the importance of making sure that core HR systems are roadworthy before setting out on the long and demanding journey of change.

This chapter has also emphasised the importance of communications, consultations and involvement in the reorganisation process, an area where HR professionals are well-qualified, perhaps uniquely, to make a strategic and tactical contribution. Here, we have emphasised the value of imagination and commitment, and particularly the role of top management to 'walk the talk' and of genuine two-way employee involvement. The evidence suggests that this pays, particularly in terms of staff retention and good employee relations. Moreover, we have emphasised the importance of communications being two-way: a source of learning as well as information. This learning theme is something we shall pursue in Chapter 5.

5 | Learning to reorganise

☐ Given the pace of contemporary reorganisations, organisations need to learn the skills and capabilities required for accomplishing repeated change.

☐ At present, learning is often embodied in the personal experience of key individuals, rather than in systematic and independent organisational capabilities.

☐ Given the commonality of basic good practice and tools, organisations should make more use of learning from external experience to improve their success in managing reorganisations.

Introduction

If the trend to shorter organisational life-cycles identified in the opening chapter continues, then one thing is sure: managers will be doing reorganisations more regularly. Already, more than half of human resource managers responding to the second survey are reporting having been involved in three or more reorganisations in the previous five years (CIPD, 2004). Reorganising is something that organisations need to learn to do.

Here, HR professionals have a critical role, both in improving their own skills and building the skills and capabilities of the organisation as a whole. From the previous chapters, we have concluded that key skills and capabilities will include confident project management, making a business case linked to an overall strategic view, and people management skills, especially in the domains of communications and consultation. It is important to ensure that these skills and capabilities are embedded thoroughly in the organisation as a whole, rather than vested exclusively in the experience of transitory consultants or a few key individuals.

Learning from inside

Sometimes, as at Nationwide and Lever Fabergé, internal consultancy or organisation effectiveness units work systematically to accumulate and disseminate internal experience in organisational change. Most organisations, however, do not have internal consultants or organisation design specialists. As shown by Figure 11, the most valued experience is that of senior managers who know the organisation well and have done reorganisations before.

Figure 11 | Key internal learning sources

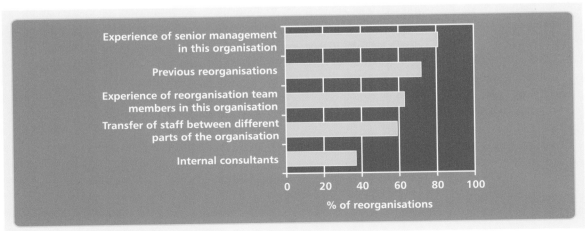

'Given the regularity of change, there is a marked reluctance to encapsulate, and then draw on, internal experience.'

Throughout the organisation, the experience of previous reorganisations is important, not just in providing a repertoire upon which to draw, but also as a means of legitimising opinions and communicating views. As in the following quotation from a manager engaged in his second change project, 'war stories' both help make change agents credible and provide an easy-to-understand reference point for important audiences:

It helps to have a war story to go into. I think it is very difficult for somebody if you haven't gone through something, if it is only book knowledge and you say [major competitor A] is doing this, or this organisation is doing this. My gut feel is that it puts people off, because the first response you get…is 'we are not [major competitor A], we are not [major competitor B]'. If you can say, 'we do this', it gives you a little bit of an edge.

Despite our overall finding of a common repertoire of basic good practice relevant across many kinds of organisations, credibility often still relies on organisation-specific knowledge. As we shall consider in the following section, external experience is often under-valued.

Moreover, as indicated in Figure 6 (on page 24), internal learning is typically highly personalised, embodied in particular individuals. Less than half of respondents to the second survey claimed to have used substantially the experience of other parts of the organisation in carrying out the particular reorganisation they were reporting on (CIPD, 2004). Only a quarter of reorganisations involved any formal internal benchmarking. Given the regularity of change, there is a marked reluctance to encapsulate, and then draw on, internal experience. Further, in light of the pace of change, and the consequent rapid accumulation of experience, organisations are surprisingly reluctant to enquire systematically and critically about the lessons from past experience. Very frequently, personal 'war stories' are the main vehicles for learning.

However, internal learning can be facilitated where there are strong internal consultancies, or their equivalents, that deliberately serve as repositories of experience (as at Nationwide or Unilever's central Organisation Effectiveness unit). Thus, Nationwide's success with the MAA reorganisation led them to employ the process of mapping methodology in other reorganisations that they are embarking upon. Learning to design the ideal account administration process has enabled Nationwide's in-house consultants to design ideal processes for all their other products.

Internal learning can, of course, happen without strong in-house consultancies, but needs management commitment and investment. As noted in Chapter 2, systematic review of completed projects is the key area in which project management widely falls short. Reorganisation projects need to budget time for continuous learning and final review right from the start. Cadbury Schweppes (see Case study 8, opposite) provides an excellent example of continuous internal learning, making use of systematic procedures and a 'no blame' culture.

Case study 8

Building in learning at Cadbury Schweppes

Cadbury Schweppes recognised the value of capturing learning from the PROBE project from the outset. In particular, the phased roll-out of the project in different regions meant that there were opportunities for improving the 'go-live' process following each successive implementation. The reorganisation team built in systematic procedures and policies for making sure that the experiences and lessons from each 'go live' were carried forward into the next.

For example, implementation managers and teams from sites that had gone through a successful implementation visited sites that were about to go through the process, to help them identify and resolve any potential issues. In addition, managers from sites that were preparing for implementation visited sites that were up and running, so they could see for themselves how the new organisation would work. Observations, lessons, and knowledge gained through the first implementation projects were documented and distilled into a change implementation handbook that was then distributed and regularly updated among change implementation teams, globally.

As well as the systematic building in of processes to capture learning, a key enabler of the learning was the fostering of a 'no-blame' culture. Instead of focusing on difficulties or challenges as negatives, these were regarded as positive action points to be shared and passed on to others who might find themselves in similar situations elsewhere in the organisation. Without this positive commitment, managers were likely to keep potential issues and problems to themselves, rather than viewing them as a challenge for the organisation and something their colleagues needed to know about.

Cadbury Schweppes' positive approach to learning is encapsulated in the advice of one senior change manager: 'Instead of asking what went wrong, ask what went right'.

Learning from outside

Existing routines and practices for carrying out reorganisations are, therefore, very important. However, reorganisations do frequently draw on external experience as well. The external benchmarking undertaken by the major retail organisation in Case study 9 provides an excellent example of systematic research. Here, the learning was considerably enhanced by the substantial use of external consultants in the change team. This organisation's experience is unusual, however. External learning in our studies tends to be highly personalised. As shown in Figure 12, on page 42, it is the personal experience of senior managers gained in other organisations that dominates. Consultants, courses and the business press are relatively neglected as potential sources of learning in reorganisations.

Case study 9

A major retail organisation: inside and outside knowledge

Learning, both internally and externally, was always regarded as a critical success factor in the head-office move that Case study 9 involved. In addition to engaging in external benchmarking, the programme director actively encouraged members of the project team to visit other organisations that had recently been through major head-office site relocations. The purpose of these visits was to gain an in-depth understanding of the practical issues and challenges that arise. As well as examining more detailed technical, logistical and operational issues relating to such things as installation of IT systems, telecommunications, building codes and health and safety regulations, the key message from these visits was the need to communicate the progress of the project to staff, and create a vision of what life in the new organisation would be like.

> '... learning from outside can be translated into meaningful internal lessons which, in turn, can be built upon in a virtuous cycle.'

Taking this learning on board, the project team set about promoting internal learning in the following ways:

◘ *Building the future*: This involved constructing mock-ups of new office spaces, workshops and design studios. Employees were then shown around these, so that they could develop a detailed impression of their new working environment.

◘ *Enacting the future*: Professional actors were commissioned to play out scenarios illustrating different kinds of behaviours, to show what would be acceptable and unacceptable in the new organisation. This included illustrating such actions as employees leaving in the middle of a meeting when their pager sounded, or colonising 'hot' desks with personal clutter.

◘ *Feedback*: Employee views on the new facilities and the new ways of working were systematically collected through questionnaires, feedback forms, the project

intranet site and at face-to-face meetings and listening groups between the project team and employee representatives. This proved invaluable for identifying issues that could potentially stall implementation.

According to the programme director of Case study 9, it pays to remember that those affected by the reorganisation can offer valuable insight into making it happen:

You say, it's all change, what do you think? What is your reaction to the furniture, the new environment, the reduction, everything? And the very fact that, you know, we're seen to be listening to people I think is very, very positive.

The experience in this case study shows that learning, both from outside and inside the organisation, helps in envisioning, designing and implementing a reorganisation. Further, learning from outside can be translated into meaningful internal lessons which, in turn, can be built upon in a virtuous cycle.

Figure 12 | Key external learning sources

'... **the embodied knowledge of consultants is often disregarded, both because of their reliance on common practices, however well tried and tested elsewhere, and their tendency to carry any learning away with them ...**'

We found senior managers to be highly confident in the value of their experience, viewing themselves as the prime carriers of expertise:

Having been involved in and worked in a very fast moving commercial organisation [food retail] for a very long period of time...there are all sorts of things that are second nature to me that are completely alien to people in this environment...I did quite a bit of stuff [in food retail] on managing change, organisational change and cultural change, coming up with innovative solutions for different things in the future. So, around that there are loads of different experiences that I have had that are totally applicable to this challenge.

Senior manager, case-study organisation

The implication is that acquiring effective change experience relies typically on recruitment. Disembodied experience is not easily trusted or absorbed.

However, even the embodied knowledge of consultants is often disregarded, both because of their reliance on common practices, however well tried and tested elsewhere, and their tendency to carry any learning away with them:

What we needed was something that recognised our unique position, specifically put together with us in mind – not an off-the-shelf package. Something that enabled the organisation to have learning and, at the end of the experience, the learning would be resident in the organisation. It wouldn't leave with the last car load of consultants who left the organisation.

Strategist, case-study organisation

The challenge for consultants seeking genuine influence on reorganisations – rather than the simple input of defined tasks – appears to be twofold. Consultants need to:

- display a range of experience from which they can tailor specific, rather than standard, solutions

- demonstrate a commitment to sharing learning with the client during the assignment.

Nevertheless, there are numerous books, models and concepts that can inform practice. Our case organisations drew on such well-known gurus as Peter Senge, Collins and Porras and JK Galbraith, who all offer frameworks that are helpful to inspiring and managing strategic change (Stanford, 2004 and Whittington and Mayer, 2002, summarise many key gurus). Beyond these, commonly used tools and methodologies in reorganisations cluster into three groups:

- specific organisation design tools such as Galbraith's 'star model' and the McKinsey 'seven Ss'

- more generic analytical tools such as simulations, process mapping and critical incident analysis

- supporting HR tools, such as competencies frameworks, job- and role-analysis methods and training needs analyses.

Practitioners often have a handful of key models that they rely upon time after time. These have been learnt either through study for MBAs or similar qualifications, through professional training as consultants or 'on the job'. Typically, the portfolio of tools is quite limited and rarely added to.

> '... a major challenge is to learn to do reorganisations differently. Change leaders are in danger of fighting the last war every time.'

Doing reorganisations differently

Given the widespread dependence on experience embodied in particular senior individuals, and the distrust of external experience from less personalised sources, a major challenge is to learn to do reorganisations differently. Change leaders are in danger of fighting the last war every time. Change routines that become embodied in senior managers are hard both to translate into generalised knowledge and to appraise systematically and critically.

The dangers of personalised routines in reorganisations are heightened by the infrequency with which reorganisations are subject to formal evaluation of whether objectives were achieved (see Figure 5 on page 16). Past experience needs to be challenged. Our first research survey asked respondents to consider what they would do differently the next time they did a reorganisation and they showed a strong willingness to learn, in principle at least (CIPD, 2003). HR professionals, with their expertise in learning and development, can make a key contribution to capturing and acting on this kind of willingness to do things differently in the future.

As Figure 13 shows, three of the most important things that respondents would devote more attention to in their next reorganisation were project management, reorganisation-related

Figure 13 | Learning from experience

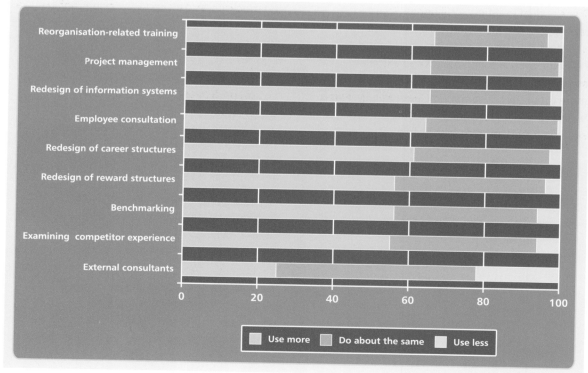

training and employee consultation. The prominence of information systems issues reinforces the point about highlighting and managing parallel changes from Chapter 2. Although they had not featured highly in the concurrent changes described in Chapter 2, features of HR management such as reward and career structures were also seen as areas to which respondents would devote more attention next time. Delayering an organisation structure, for example, can have a major impact on pay and career structures and the effects need to be considered and addressed. There was, however, a marked general reluctance to make more use of external consultants. Consultants are not a source of learning that reorganisation practitioners are eager to pursue further.

Conclusions

There is clearly a strong willingness to learn to reorganise more effectively, in particular in the areas of project management, training and consultation. After all, reorganisations are something that managers have to do more and more often. At the same time, however, there is a widespread failure to undertake this learning in a systematic and independent fashion.

Reorganisation projects are often not appraised rigorously after completion; consultants are distrusted; benchmarking and external learning are relatively neglected.

This lack of systematic learning can easily leave reorganisations in the hands of a few key individuals with past experience. Given the commonality of good basic practices between organisations and sectors, this experience is likely to be relevant and helpful. However, 'war stories' are, by definition, about old wars. The personal experience of key managers is hard to interrogate critically and not easily shared with others. If organisations wish to improve their skills and capabilities in managing reorganisations, they need to invest properly in learning, especially from outside and elsewhere in their organisation. They need, moreover, to ensure that this learning is rigorously appraised and accessible, both systematically and independently, throughout the organisation. Learning will have to become the property of organisations rather than individuals and, given their knowledge and expertise in this area, it is another key aspect of the contribution that HR professionals can make to successful reorganisations.

6 | Summary and implications for HR practice and development

Introduction

This report has identified regular reorganising as an inescapable feature of contemporary management. These reorganisations should not be dismissed as tiresome distractions from real business, but as having strategic importance for the organisation as a whole. Reorganisations are particularly important for HR professionals. In terms of reorganisation outcomes, employee-related areas are the greatest source of failure. At the same time, more than any other function, HR professionals are being drawn into influential roles in reorganisations. Rather than simply picking up the human consequences of reorganisations after the event, HR professionals are taking increasingly substantial roles as shapers of change.

Drawing on experience from eleven case studies from the private, public and voluntary sectors, together with responses from nearly 1,500 surveyed managers, this Report proposes a basic repertoire of good reorganisation practices that are potentially relevant across a wide range of organisations and sectors. These practices need to be drawn upon discriminatingly, but across the researched organisations as a whole they are generally associated with superior performance outcomes. Together, they offer a tested checklist of factors relevant to the practice of successful organising. They also have implications for how human resource professionals manage their own training and development.

Successful organising

An orientating device throughout this Report has been the 'seven steps to successful organising'. These 'seven steps' highlight the factors that most clearly differentiate successful from unsuccessful reorganisations, as identified from the second survey. The case studies provide more detail with

which to elaborate these 'seven steps' and, indeed, the two surveys identify other factors important to success, but which less successful reorganisations may be using rightly, too. The 'seven steps', therefore, provide a basic framework to which other factors can be added. Here, we summarise them and draw out the implications for HR professionals.

1 Sustained top-management support

The first item in the 'seven steps' is sustained top-management support. The second survey established personal commitment and political support on the part of top management as a crucial differentiator between success and failure in reorganisations. Our case studies concur, with considerable effort devoted, typically, not only to engaging top management in the formal governance mechanisms, but involving them personally through events such as the United Utilities away-days or the Ordnance Survey Experience. Critical, here, is the ability to commit top management through a well-developed strategic business case. Also important will be the need to re-engage top management as circumstances inevitably change during the course of the reorganisation, as in the case of PROBE at Cadbury Schweppes with its major acquisition. Senior HR professionals need to be represented at this level, to assert and demonstrate the criticality of the people-management agenda to senior executive colleagues. Their skills are also called upon to manage the sensitive political processes that major changes typically involve.

2 Coherent change

Making a strategic business case and keeping top management aboard both link to the second of the 'seven steps', the assembling of a coherent change programme. Any single reorganisation

'... managers ranked information systems as the top item they would attend to more in their next reorganisation project.'

initiative has to move in step with a broader and changing strategic agenda. The reorganisation itself will have implications for a wide range of aspects of the business. Parallel changes in accounting and control systems and in business processes emerge as particularly strongly associated with superior financial outcomes. Looking back on past experience, managers ranked information systems as the top item they would attend to more in their next reorganisation project. HR professionals also need to ensure that consideration is given at an early stage to the people management component of the reorganisation:

◘ How will we involve people and develop their support?

◘ What will be the effect on reward systems and how can we use them to promote, rather than obstruct, the necessary changes?

◘ What job and skill changes will be required and how will we deliver them?

◘ What are the implications for the careers of those affected by and managing the reorganisation?

◘ How will we continually learn and improve as we implement the reorganisation?

3   Substantive involvement

The third step that differentiates successful from unsuccessful reorganisations is substantive employee involvement and consultation. Organisations are nearly all doing a great deal in terms of communicating information and explaining change, but it is involvement that makes the crucial difference. Again, this is one of

the very top items change managers would devote more attention to in their next reorganisation. The employee relations and involvement knowledge and skills of HR professionals can help to generate the necessary improvements in this field. Involvement makes communications two-way, a source of learning about the reorganisation's shape and progress. It builds understanding, acceptance and ownership. Involvement can range from formal representation procedures, as at CACHE, through to less structured feedback or question-and-answer sessions. Organisations should not take for granted employees' ability to participate in involvement activities. As at United Utilities, for example, it may be worthwhile to invest in training employees how to deliver feedback. Tokenistic or unsustained involvement can easily engender counter-productive cynicism.

4   Communications

The fourth step differentiating between successful and unsuccessful reorganisations is investment in communications, especially external communications. Externally, suppliers, customers and financial stakeholders, are critical. Internally, communications with employees need to be multi-channel, potentially going beyond simple written media. Communications should be multi-directional too, embracing top management and line managers as key conduits of information and essential supporters of change. Communications, however, are likely to involve a substantial commitment: as at Lever Fabergé, there may be as many as 26 distinct audiences involved. HR professionals are key to securing the time and resources to make communication effective. CIPD research suggests that around one-third of HR departments are now responsible for internal communications, and in other cases they are working closely with communication professionals to plan and deliver the right information in the right way to staff (CIPD, 2003). In playing a role as guardian of the company culture, HR professionals are also running staff surveys before, during and after reorganisations, facilitating the upward communication that is a crucial source of learning and engagement.

5   HR staff involvement

A consistent theme in this report has been the importance of HR professionals getting heavily and directly engaged in reorganisations as shapers of change. Senior HR professionals are typically closely involved in major reorganisations at least every couple of years. HR professionals are rated by chief executives as the most important source of advice and learning with regard to reorganisations. Having good people-management skills in a reorganisation team strongly differentiates between successful and unsuccessful reorganisations, and developing these is another key contribution of the HR function. Involvement of HR professionals in project steering groups or management teams positively impacts on a range of performance outcomes, especially employee-related items such as retention and morale. HR professionals have to regard reorganisation as a key part of their job.

6   Project management

The sixth step differentiating between successful and unsuccessful reorganisations is good project management. Reorganisations need organising too. As at Nationwide, for instance, project management disciplines and skills should be thoroughly embedded in the organisation as a whole. Project management is being practised widely in the United Kingdom, but end-of-project reviews and evaluations are often skipped.

Investing more in project management is at the top of the list of items that experienced change managers would do in their next reorganisation, and HR professionals need to demonstrate the case for such investment and then deliver the development of the requisite skills. At the same time, project management in itself is not a cure-all, and managers should guard against letting project management procedures become rigid and cumbersome in rapidly changing circumstances.

7   Skilled teams

The final step is assembling a reorganisation team with the right skills and experience. A major differentiator between successful and unsuccessful reorganisations is the level of team skills in both project management and people management. Recalling Lever Fabergé's case example, even a team made up of skilled individuals cannot be assumed to work well just by itself: teams need bonding together to work as effective units. There should also be a clear post-project pathway for team members: as at United Utilities, participation in change teams can be made part of a career trajectory to senior line-management positions. Moreover, skills and experience should not be allowed to become too personalised. Using end-of-project reviews and similar devices, managers should ensure that reorganisation skills are being built systematically into the organisation as a whole, rather than residing in a few powerful, and possibly mobile, individuals. Team-building competencies are a well-established and core area for HR professionals, and demonstrate that there is no clear divide between the tactical and transformational in terms of how they can add significant value to reorganisations and improve the chances of success.

'Our research highlights the tremendous opportunities for HR professionals to make a major contribution to improving the experiences and outcomes of reorganisations.'

Developing successful practitioners

It is clear that HR professionals need to be ready to step up to the challenge of reorganisations. There are specific benefits in terms of employee-related outcomes, such as morale and key staff retention. But reorganisations are also more successful in terms of broader efficiency and effectiveness where HR professionals are closely involved.

The skills and capabilities required for organising are challenging, nevertheless. They certainly involve function-specific expertise – core HR activities such as resourcing, training and development and reward. However, the skills and capabilities for successful organising go beyond this functional expertise to include process skills, such as project management and facilitation; organisation design skills, such as those embodied in the McKinsey 'seven Ss'; and strategic skills, in the sense of being able to situate and coordinate a reorganisation project within the broader and shifting strategic agenda of the organisation as a whole. Acquiring these skills and capabilities has substantial implications for the training and development of HR professionals.

HR professionals seeking more influential roles in reorganisations need to build on top of a solid foundation of core HR technical knowledge and practice, and a wider set of experiences. They will need to be confident in making a strategic business case; ready to contribute outside their core expertise to project teams drawn from a range of disciplines; proficient with a wide range of process, design and business tools; and

cosmopolitan in their openness to experience and learning from outside their own organisation. All this implies training and careers that are likely to extend beyond those available within a particular organisation or a single function. HR professionals capable of shaping change often pursue 'zig-zag' careers that take them through a range of organisations, training and functions, while constantly referring back to and updating their core expertise, ie people managing. Correspondingly, line and change managers from other disciplines need to develop greater understanding and knowledge in people management.

HR professionals also have a broader responsibility that goes beyond their ability to contribute directly to particular reorganisations. In today's conditions of relentless reorganising, it is a key part of the HR professional's role to build the wider capacity of their organisations to change. Organisations need the widespread capacity to work in disciplined project teams, to coordinate between functions and business units and to learn systematically from internal and external experience. Senior HR professionals will have to ensure that change skills and capabilities are embedded in their organisations as wholes, as well as in their own particular functions. Our research highlights the tremendous opportunities for HR professionals to make a major contribution to improving the experiences and outcomes of reorganisations. With this research we hope we have contributed to more of them having the knowledge, tools and capabilities to deliver on that potential.

References

CHARTERED INSTITUTE OF PERSONNEL AND DEVELOPMENT (2003)

HR Survey: Where we are, where we're heading. London: Chartered Institute of Personnel and Development.

CHARTERED INSTITUTE FOR PERSONNEL AND DEVELOPMENT (2003)

Reorganising for Success: CEOs' and HR Managers' Perceptions. London: Chartered Institute of Personnel and Development.

CHARTERED INSTITUTE FOR PERSONNEL AND DEVELOPMENT (2004)

Reorganising for Success: a Survey of HR's Role in Change. London: Chartered Institute of Personnel and Development.

D'AVENI, R. and THOMAS, L. (2005)

'The Rise of Hyper Competition from 1950 to 2002: Evidence of Increasing Structural Destabilization and Temporary Competitive Advantage'. Working paper. Place: University of Dartmouth.

DAY, J. (2001)

'Organising for Growth'. *McKinsey Quarterly*. 2, 4–6.

HUTCHINSON, J. (2005)

'Case Study: Ordnance Survey'. *People Management*. 5 April, 39.

LEAVITT, H. (2003)

'Why Hierarchies Thrive'. *Harvard Business Review*. March, 97–102.

MIRANDA, S. (2005)

'Creating the Indispensable HR Function'. *Strategic HR Review*. 4, 3, 32–35.

MOLLOY, E. and WHITTINGTON, R. (2004)

HR: Making Change Happen. London: Chartered Institute of Personnel and Development.

MOLLOY, E. and WHITTINGTON, R. (2005)

'Organising Organising: the Practice inside the Process'. *Advances in Strategic Management*. (forthcoming)

OXMAN, J. and SMITH, B. (2003)

'The Limits of Structural Change'. *MIT Sloan Management Review*. 45, 1, 77–82.

PETTIGREW, A. and WHITTINGTON, R. (2001)

'Managing "Joined Up" Change'. *People Management*. 11 October, 52–54.

STANFORD, N. (2004)

Organization Design: the Collaborative Approach. Oxford: Butterworth-Heinemann.

WHITTINGTON, R. and MAYER, M. (2002)

Organising for Success in the Twenty-First Century: A Starting Point for Change. London: Chartered Institute of Personnel and Development.

WHITTINGTON, R. (2004)

'Strategy after Modernism: Recovering Practice'. *European Management Review*. 1, 1: 62–68.

WHITTINGTON, R., MOLLOY, M., MAYER, M., SMITH, A. and FENTON, E. (2005)

'Communicate, communicate, communicate – that's how change managers succeed'. *People Management*. 7 April, 38–42.